GODLY INSPIRATIONAL LOVE

ALICE FAYE LUCAS

Copyright © 2016 by Alice Faye Lucas

Godly Inspirational Love
by Alice Faye Lucas

Printed in the United States of America.

ISBN 9781498482448

All rights reserved solely by the author. The author guarantees all contents are original and do not infringe upon the legal rights of any other person or work. No part of this book may be reproduced in any form without the permission of the author. The views expressed in this book are not necessarily those of the publisher.

www.xulonpress.com

This book is lovingly dedicated to Jesus, my Lord and Savior, who inspires me to write and my family and friends who have loved and supported me down through the years.

Table of Contents

A Beacon In The Night 15
A Branch Of Jesus 16
A Branch Of Jesus The Vine 17
A Child Of Love 18
A Child Of The King 19
A Christmas Ode 20
A Favorite Hiding Place 21
A Flame Of Love 22
A Follower Of The King 23
A Fountain Flowing Free 24
A Gift So Free 25
A Haven Of Peace 26
A Little Bird On Wing 27
Amazing Grace Made Me Whole 28
Amazing Love 29
A Melody That Never Stops 30
A Song Within My Heart 31
An Angel In My Pocket 32
An Angel Of My Own 33
Angel Of Mine 34
A Perfect Haven Of Rest 35
A Perfect Time For Prayer 36
A Precious Hiding Place 37

A Special Angel	38
A Spirit Has Flown Away	39
Awesome Is Our God	40
Back To The Country	41
Be A Blessing	42
Be A Blessing For Jesus	43
Because Of You Lord	44
Become More Like Jesus	45
Believe And Trust In Jesus	46
Believe In God	47
Beyond The Sunset	48
Blessings From Above	49
Blessings Galore	50
Butterflies	51
Butterflies Are Beautiful	52
Butterflies At Play	53
Call On Jesus	54
Call Unto Jesus	55
Choose To Follow Jesus	56
Christmas In Heaven	57
Christmas Night's Delight	58
Christmas Time	59
Claim Jesus As Your Own	60
Delivered From Darkness	61
Draw Me Nearer To Thee	62
Faith	63
Flowers Lift Our Spirit High	64
Follow Jesus	65
Give God Control	66
Glorify God	67
God Calls Us All	68
God Can Change You	69
God Carries Us On	70
God Excels In Mercy And Grace	71
God Fills My Soul With Joyful Glee	72
God Holds Us In His Loving Caress	73
God Is Awesome In His Powers	74

Table of Contents

God Is Faithful And Just 75
God Is Majestic 76
God Is Our Father 77
God Is Our Shining Star 78
God Lends His Love 79
God Looks Out For You 80
God Loves You 81
God Of Love 82
God Rescues Us 83
God Sends Angels 84
God Sends The Rainbow 85
God Sent Me An Angel 86
God Shines His Love Light 87
God Touched Me 88
God's Gifts 89
God's Grace 90
God's Hands 91
God's Love 92
God's Love Is Genuine 93
God's Presence 94
God's Promices 95
God's Redeeming Love 96
God's Voice 97
God Will Deliver Us 98
Grace 99
Grace And Mercy 100
Grief Is Only Temporary 101
Heal Our Nation Lord 102
Hearld Angels Are Singing 103
Heaven's Land 104
I Am Yours And You Are Mine 105
I Belong To Jesus 106
I Can Only Imagine 107
I Claim Jesus As My Own 109
I Cherish My Redeemers Love 110
I Dreamed Of Heaven 111
If I Could Never Pray 112

Godly Inspirational Love

If Only	113
In Christ I Stand	114
I Need You Lord	115
I Praise You Lord	116
I Seek After You Lord	117
I Sing Unto My King	118
I Want To Follow You Lord	119
I Want To Kneel At God's Throne	120
I Want To See God	121
I Want To See Jesus	122
I Will Follow You Lord	123
I Will Gladly Follow Jesus	124
I Will Never Walk Alone	125
Jesus And Me	126
Jesus Assures That You're Blest	127
Jesus' Awesome Love	128
Jesus Can Make You Whole	129
Jesus Died For Our Sins	130
Jesus Draws You Close To Him	131
Jesus Gives Eternal Rest	132
Jesus Gives Salvation And Eternal Life	133
Jesus' Glory And Grace	134
Jesus, Greatest Name I Know	135
Jesus' Hand In Mine	136
Jesus Is Always Near	137
Jesus Is Easy To Find	138
Jesus Is In Control	139
Jesus Is King Of All Kings	140
Jesus Is My Comforter	141
Jesus Is King	142
Jesus Is My King	143
Jesus Is My Righteousness	144
Jesus Is Our King	145
Jesus Is Our Savior	146
Jesus Is The Answer	147
Jesus Is The Atoning Sacrifice	148
Jesus Is The Morning Star	149

Table of Contents

Jesus Is The Reason For The Season 150
Jesus Is There For You And Me 151
Jesus Knocked On My Hearts Door 152
Jesus Lifts Me Up 153
Jesus Lives Deep Within Our Heart 154
Jesus' Love 155
Jesus Makes All Things New 156
Jesus Offers Eternity 157
Jesus, Our Lord, Takes Away Sin 158
Jesus Paid For Our Sins 159
Jesus' Promise 160
Jesus Purchased My Redemption 161
Jesus, Son Of God 162
Jesus Stands By Us 163
Jesus Took Me In 164
Jesus Touched Me 165
Jesus Transformed My Soul 166
Jesus Watches Over Me 167
Jesus Will Carry You On 168
Jesus Will Mend Our Broken Ways 169
Jesus Will See You Through 170
Jesus Will Never Let You Down 171
Jesus Will Rescue You 172
Jesus Will Revive Us Again 173
Jesus Will See You Through 174
Kneel In Prayer 175
Lamb Of God, My Prince Of Peace 176
Let Jesus Come Into Your Heart 177
Let Love Reign 178
Life Is Fleeting 179
Lift Me Up Lord 180
Little Hummingbird 181
Lock Jesus Within Your Heart 182
Longing For Heaven 183
Lord, Direct My Path 184
Lord, Draw Me Near 185
Lord, Help Me Make It Through 186

Lord, I Need You... 187
Lord, Reveal Thine Own Way 188
Love So Awesome And True............................... 189
Love That Serves You Well................................. 190
Magnify The Lord... 191
Majestic Beauty Of Snow.................................... 192
Marvelous Grace.. 193
Missing Mom 194
More Like Thee Lord 195
My Beacon In The Night 196
My Blessings From God...................................... 197
My Father, God.. 198
My Greatest Sensation 199
My Guiding Light... 200
My Heart With Rapture Soars............................. 201
My Heart's Song... 202
My Hope And Salvation 203
My Lord And King 204
My Master, Redeemer And Friend 205
My Own Earthly Angel....................................... 206
My Salvation.. 207
My Savior Will Never Forsake Me...................... 208
My Savior's Love 209
My Secret Hiding Place 210
No, I'm Not Dead 211
Only God Is Worthy Of Praise 212
On The Wings Of A Dove................................... 213
Open My Eyes Lord 214
Open My Eyes Lord And Let Me See.................. 215
Our Heavenly Home... 216
Our Only Salvation 217
Our Shield And Defender 218
Our Source Of Salvation Is Jesus 219
Praise And Glorify God 220
Praise God In His Diety 221
Promise Of Eternity 222
Rely On Jesus 223

Table of Contents

Revived With A Spiritual Flame 224
Salvation Free 225
Salvations Plan 226
Satisfied With Jesus. 227
Saved By Grace. 228
Saved By His Grace 229
Seek His Face 230
Seek Jesus 231
She Is Not Dead 232
Sheltered In God's Grace 233
Sheltered In God's Love 234
Shirley Is Not Gone 235
Show Me Sweet Jesus. 236
Show Me The Way Lord. 237
Sing Of Jesus' Birth 238
Sing Unto God 239
Someday Soon 240
Songs In The Night. 241
Spring Is Here. 242
Stay Near Me Lord 243
Surrender To The Lord 244
Sweet Eternity. 245
Sweet Holy Spirit 246
Thankful For The Lamb 247
Thanking God For Salvation. 248
The Angel Band 249
The Divine Bridge. 250
The Greatest Friend Ever Known 251
The Heavenly Stairway. 252
The Journey To Heaven 253
The Keeper Of My Heart 254
The Lord Is My Everything 255
The Lord Is My Hope For Eternity. 256
The Master Of Divinity. 257
The Soul Shall Never Die 258
The Touch Of His Hand 259
The Whippoorwills 260

There Is Peace With Jesus................................261
Throw Out The Lifeline 262
Trust God 263
Unchanging Love 264
Walk With Me Lord 265
Walk Within God's Light Of Love 266
We Belong To God 267
What A Glorious Day 268
When I Am Gone 269
Wings Of Love 270
Worship Jesus In His Deity.............................271
Worship The Almighty King Of Kings..................272
Your Lifeline Crutch...................................273
Your Redeemer And Friend 274

A BEACON IN THE NIGHT

Lord stay within my sight
Shine on me your perfect light
Be my beacon in the night.

Shine your love on me
Help me share it free
And lead the lost to thee.

Give me the words to say
To help others find the way
Into your heavenly fold today.

Thank you Jesus for saving my soul
Your amazing love has made me whole
My life, my all you now control.

You guided me from darkness to light
You're my beacon in the night
Your countenance shines forever bright.

Sweet Jesus, a beacon for you I'll be
So all others I meet may look and see
I live only to glorify thee!

A BRANCH OF JESUS

I know Jesus shall forever be mine
For I am a branch of Him, the vine
He has tied me next to Him with holy twine.

Jesus will never leave me alone
He has claimed me as His own
He's the greatest friend I've ever known.

Jesus is my Redeemer who loves me so
He is with me no matter where I go
He lifts me up when I'm sinking low.

I'm a branch of Jesus, the vine
He blesses my life thru love divine
To let me know His love is genuine!

A BRANCH OF JESUS THE VINE

I am a branch of Jesus, the Vine
I shall remain in Him as forever mine
For I know His love is genuine.

Apart from Jesus there's nothing I can do
I shall remain in Him my entire life through
He's my Redeemer who died my life to renew.

Jesus shelters me in His arms of love
He lifts my heart to Him above
He flies my troubles away as if on wings of a dove.

As a branch of Jesus I will thrive and grow
In His amazing love that He doth bestow
And I shall bask forever in the beauty of the afterglow!

A CHILD OF LOVE

Long ago on Christmas morn
A child of love was born.
Hallelujahs rang out from the sky
As herald angels praised him from on high.

He's Jesus, our Savior Lord and King
Great tidings to earth He did bring.
He gave His life to ransom you and me
Because of Him salvation is now free.

Living He loved us; dying He gave salvations plan
Although He was perfect, He died for His fellowman.
Love like His has never been expressed before
His grace and mercy paved our way to heaven's door!

A CHILD OF THE KING

I am so thankful to be a child of the King
Heavenly Father, great joy to life you bring.
I shall worship you all of my days
As my most high God who shall rule always.

Father, God, thank you for staying near
When I call on you I know you'll always hear.
You're a miraculous God whose love will never end
The keeper of my heart and my most cherished friend.

Savior of mine, you constantly shed your glory on me
To show me exactly what you want me to be.
Yea' I'm thankful to be a child of you, the King
You give my soul a reason to joyfully sing!

A CHRISTMAS ODE

Hope and joy Christmas day doth bring
It's the day that God sent us His Son, Jesus, the King
Let peace and love throughout these lands ring!

Angelic voices praise His birth with wings unfurled
He was sent to redeem a lost and dying world
All our sin and shame on Him was hurled!

Glorify and praise Him on bended knee
Our sins were nailed to the cross with Him at Calvary
So that someday we may live again and forever ransomed be!

A FAVORITE HIDING PLACE

There's a favorite hiding place
Within the arms of Jesus
Wrapped in His warm embrace.

When I'm troubled and can't cope
Within His loving arms
He gives me wondrous hope.

I know deep within my heart
I can always call on Him
His awesome love to impart.

Yea' Jesus will hold me tight
And make things right,
As He whispers softly to me
Awesome words of sweet eternity.

Jesus provides His favorite hiding place
Within His amazing love and grace.
I'm so glad I opened my heart to let Him in
He took away all my heartache and sin!

A FLAME OF LOVE

When all your dreams have been overthrown
And you feel lost and all alone,
Jesus sees you in your deep, dark despair
Just call on Him and He'll meet you there.

At times it's easy to lose all hope
And feel like you've reached the end of your rope.
Fortunately, there is a Savior above
Whose heart is filled with awesome love.

All you have to do is pray from the depths of your heart
Jesus stands ready to intervene and do His part.
He will light your path on the darkest night
And illuminate your soul with His divine light.

Jesus' flame of love will rekindle your heart and mind
As He draws you near with chords that bind.
He keeps His flame of love ever so near
To share with His children who to Him are dear.

So when things seem hopelessly dark and dim
Cling to His promises and call on Him.
Kneel down and pray to our Savior above
He will flood your heart and soul with His love!

A FOLLOWER OF THE KING

I am a follower of Christ the King
He means more to me than anything
Great joy to my life He doth bring.

Jesus is my Savior and the keeper of my soul
He came into my life and took control
His amazing love has made me whole.

I am glad Jesus claimed me as His own
He is the greatest friend I have ever known
I will follow Him from now on.

Yea' I am a follower of the King
He makes my heart joyfully sing
And my steps lightly spring!

A FOUNTAIN FLOWING FREE

There's a fountain flowing free
With living water for eternity
That Jesus offers to you and me.

It will satisfy needs from the start
As it becomes a vital part
Deep down inside our heart.

God's grace will cure our vilest sin
If we will let His glory shine to our heart within
It will make us happier than we've ever been.

Come drink of this fountain today
The Saviors touch will take all guilt away
And put you on the heavenly pathway!

A GIFT SO FREE

Sinner, did you know
That Jesus loves you so?
He freely chose to die
For sinners like you and I.

He died nailed to a cross
So our soul wouldn't be lost.
He suffered pain and humiliation
Just to give us Salvation.

His gift to us is free
Our souls can forever ransomed be.
Accept His gift and the blessings He has in store
His amazing love opens the path to heaven's door!

A HAVEN OF PEACE

There's a Haven of rest beyond the sky
Far above the silver clouds on high
There the soul shall never die.

If we trust in Jesus and His amazing grace
When this life is over and we end our earthly race
We'll meet Him there face to face.

Our day may come to go before too long
Angels will greet us there in joyful song
And we'll be with Jesus exactly where we belong.

We shall gather around Gods holy throne
And He shall claim us as His own
No greater joy have we ever known.

Dear God, help us make our final earthly stand
To enter thy blessed promised land
Heaven is our goal and Jesus is our brand.

We'll walk streets of gold with Jesus hand in hand
As we glorify him as King of all Kings in His celestial land
Where peace will reign free and love is forever grand!

A LITTLE BIRD ON WING

Today I watched a little bird on wing
As he landed near my window to merrily sing
Oh' what joy to my heart he did bring.

As his notes rang out with not a flaw
I watched and listened to him in awe
And on the beauty of his tune I did draw.

God in his infinite wisdom created him
With a song in his throat that would overwhelm
And brighten the days when dark and grim.

He sings to God, his maker, of all creation
In his only way of communication
With heartfelt love and dedication!

AMAZING GRACE MADE ME WHOLE

Dear Lord, I know you hear my every prayer
And keep me safely sheltered in thy care.
I am so happy to be a cherished part of you
Your love always comes to my rescue.

Lord, I love you with all my heart and soul
Your amazing grace has made me whole.
When I am tired and weary you intervene
And on your everlasting arms I safely lean.

Lord, I marvel at thy works and see how great thy art
You gave me life anew with a brand new start.
I'll forever worship you and your winsome ways
One thing is sure; I'll always give you highest praise!

AMAZING LOVE

Lord, your love is amazing and free
All we have to do is trust and believe in thee.
Within our life you take complete control
And give us grace to redeem our soul.

Lord, we wouldn't know what to do
If not for the awesome love of you.
Life would have no meaning and be bleak
So it's your loving ways we constantly seek.

Lord, when our days turn dark and dim
Your love light shines to overwhelm.
You are the sunshine and joy in our life
As Master and Redeemer you take away our strife!

A MELODY THAT NEVER STOPS

There's a melody I continuously sing
Within my heart the notes joyfully ring
Acknowledging Jesus as Lord, Savior and King.

My melody stays in tune and never stops
Within my heart it stays sweet and is always tops
When I am stressed or burdened out it pops.

Jesus implanted the melody to forever stay
So thru divine love He could bless me each day
And keep me in His sight so I wouldn't go astray!

A SONG WITHIN MY HEART

There's a song within this heart of mine
Telling me God's love is genuine.
He holds me close with the notes ringing
His love keeps me forever softly singing.

God walks close beside me each day
He keeps me from wandering and going astray.
Within our hearts we sing the sweet song
As hand in hand we stroll along.

God gave me the song that I sing
He blessed me with the joy that it doth bring.
It tells of His awesome mercy and love
And His wondrous blessings He sends from above!

AN ANGEL IN MY POCKET

I have an angel in my pocket
Yes, it's really true.
My angel in my pocket
Watches over all that I do.

When I stray away from the Lord
He rescues me in sweet accord,
And lends His healing rays
To mend my broken ways.

My little angel keeps me on the go
And is quick to let me know,
God's glory must forever shine
Within this heart and soul of mine.

My pocket angel is commanded
By God from Heaven above,
To display His mercy and kindness
And keep me sheltered in His love!

AN ANGEL OF MY OWN

Lord, give me an angel to lean on
A precious little angel to claim as my own
So I'll never have to face life alone.

Place my angel deep within my heart and soul
So when life gets tough and storm clouds roll
My own little angel can intervene and take control.

Lord, fill my angel with thy pure sweet love
So he can guide me heavenward to you above
And rescue me when others push and shove!

ANGEL OF MINE

You are an angel empowered by God's grace divine
Your loving ways and actions are genuine
I am so glad you're a special angel of mine.

All you have to do is cast your healing rays
To revive my spirit and mend my broken ways
Your awesome love always blesses my days.

You are an angel whose love is forever true
You know exactly how to cheer me when I'm blue
And change my entire point of view.

God always knows exactly what I need
He sends you, angel of mine, to intercede
So my hungry soul you may feed!

A PERFECT HAVEN OF REST

There's a land of beauty and wondrous allure
It's a place of peace and rest where the soul shall forever endure
The skies are never cloudy and the air is fresh and pure.

Jesus patiently waits at those pearly gates to welcome us in
To that perfect haven of rest where there is no sin
And a new life with Christ our Savior we will begin.

We'll sing and shout with the angel band
In that beautiful far away land
And we shall live eternally under God's command!

A PERFECT TIME FOR PRAYER

In the early morn
When day is being reborn,
Dew drops gleam like diamonds in the sun
And are such beautiful sights to look upon.

It is a perfect time for heartfelt prayer
As I thank God for His love and care.
All around me is quiet and still
Except for the mocking birds sweet twill.

He begins singing at the break of dawn
As he cheerfully hops across my lawn.
Spring time breezes pervade the air
Filling my senses with joy and cheer.

The heavens smile down at me
My heart dances wild and free.
The dawning holds great ecstasy
As I praise God on bended knee!

A PRECIOUS HIDING PLACE

There's a precious hiding place
It's within the balm of God's grace.
The presence of the Holy Spirit is there
And His majestic love lingers near.

Enter God's hiding place this very day
He will take all of your guilt away.
His grace is greater than all your sin
He'll give you peace deep within.

God's grace and mercy never ends
Daily His amazing love to us He lends.
Be grateful for the blessings He gives
And praise Him as our King who forever lives!

A SPECIAL ANGEL

A special angel to heaven has flown
Yet precious memories of him shall linger on
Of the deeds of kindness to others he has shown.

He had a gift of giving and witnessing to everyone
And relayed the message of God and His Redeeming Son
Now the final course on this earthly life He has run.

His spirit soared to heaven as if on wings of a dove
He leaves with us a precious legacy of love
That God, His Father, endowed to him from above.

We will desperately miss him I know
But shall always rejoice in the beauty of his afterglow
And feel his presence as through life we go!

A SPIRIT HAS FLOWN AWAY

Our hearts are deeply saddened
In losing our earthly friend.
Yet our souls are suddenly gladdened
Just in knowing this is not the end.

Her spirit has only flown away
To her heavenly home and a much fairer day.
She's met Jesus, her Savior face to face
There she shall be sheltered in His grace.

She's placed her hand in Jesus' nail scarred hand
And now sings in exaltation with the angel band.
She smiles sweetly from Heavens Land
Where mercy is great and grace is grand.

Soon our spirit will joyfully fly
To meet her above the silver clouds on high.
She waits patiently for you and me
To join her there where we shall live eternally!

AWESOME IS OUR GOD

Our God is an awesome God
He works miracles every day.
Though your path be dark and dreary
He stands available to show you the way.

God is bigger than your heartaches
He goes before you and a way makes.
He oversees all, overlooks none
He abides with you until your course is run.

God will cleanse your soul your spirit to renew
He gives pure thoughts and a clean heart too.
He provides holiness, strength and power
Bountiful blessings on you He doth shower.

Believe in Him and follow His command
Reach out and grasp His nail scarred hand.
He will lead you to Heaven's land
Were you shall make your final stand!

BACK TO THE COUNTRY

Take me back to the country
Where meadows are so green
And the soft breezes blow
It's there I long to go.

I want to walk the land
Where I used to run and play,
And roam the fields and woodlands
As I did on a long ago day.

I long to hear the birds sing
In notes that joyfully ring,
And follow the brook that gently flows
In the forest where the weeping willow grows.

I'll feast my eyes upon the beautiful wild flowers
And feel the falling rain that comes in showers.
I want to lie beneath the old oak tree
And relive precious moments of tranquility.

Back to the country I long to go
Where life is tranquil and slow
To watch the setting suns majestic glow
It's the only Heaven on earth that I know!

BE A BLESSING

Be a blessing for Gods glorification
Expand on His gift of free Salvation.
Witness to others and tell them of His love
Win souls for Jesus; direct them to heaven above.

Being a blessing is not an easy thing to do
God stands ready and available to help you.
Ask Him to take you out of the bondage of sin
His glory He is always ready to shine in.

Make peace with Jesus thru the blood of His cross
His grace is sufficient to assure you do not suffer loss.
Bring glory to Him and surrender to His perfect will
Submit in faith to God; He'll make your heart quiet and still.

Jesus loved you before you loved Him
He paved your way to the heavenly realm.
Place your heart and soul in His hands
Believe in Him and follow His commands!

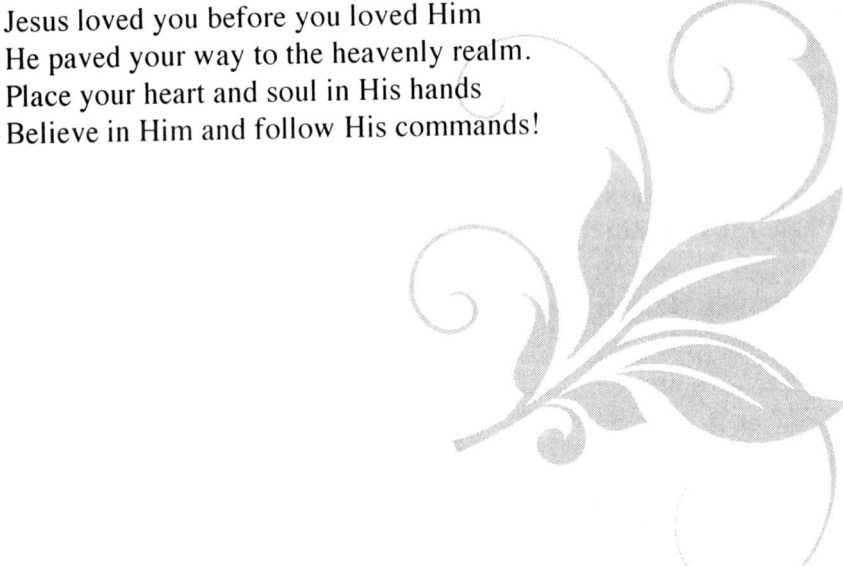

BE A BLESSING FOR JESUS

Believe in Jesus to save you
Your heart and soul He will renew.
His loving ways He will impart
And give you a brand new start.

Trust in Jesus without delay
He will change your darkest night to day.
Your empty cup He will fill to the brim
And your greatest desire will be to live for Him.

Worship Jesus and give Him praise
He stands ready to mend your broken ways.
Grace and love He renders at the start
He'll shape your life and reform your heart.

Become a blessing for Jesus' glory today
He will take all your transgressions away.
His love will transform your heart forever
And bind you next to Him with chords no man can sever!

BECAUSE OF YOU LORD

Lord, because of what you have done
Victory over sin I have won.
Because of what you are to me
My soul shall forever ransomed be.

Lord, because of thy love and majesty
You died on the cross to redeem me.
I know that I am nothing without thee
Bind me next to you with threads of love for eternity.

Lord, because I know your love is true
I dedicate my heart and soul to you.
Lift my broken spirit high above the skies
Where I shall reign with you forever in paradise!

BECOME MORE LIKE JESUS

Take up your cross and follow Jesus
He is the way, the truth and the light.
Live your life the way He lived
Trust in Him with all your might.

Kneel before Jesus in heartfelt prayer
Place you burdens in His care.
He, your Master and Redeemer, will set you free
Over sin and shame, He offers victory.

Exalt Christ and experience the joy it brings
He'll wrap you in His arms of love,
And hold you tight until your heart with rapture sings
Your troubles will fly away as if on wings.

Become more like Jesus; emulate His ways
He is worthy of your glorification and praise.
He will take away the hardened parts of your heart
His grace and love within your life He will impart!

BELIEVE AND TRUST IN JESUS

In this world of constant turmoil
Are you diligently searching for peace?
Jesus is the answer my friend
He can give you sweet release.

God hung the stars, moon and sun
He created the universe and rules it today.
His Son, Jesus, He sent to earth to redeem you and me
Jesus died on the cross to take our sins away.

We only have to believe and trust in Him
He will guide us to His heavenly realm.
Lift your heart to Him and pray
He will keep you on the straight and narrow way!

BELIEVE IN GOD

Believe in God and follow His will
Listen for His voice; be quiet and still.
He'll guide your steps if you believe
His blessed promises you'll receive.

God will live within your heart
And become a main and vital part,
In guiding your actions night and day
He'll hear your prayers when you pray.

God is awesome and powerful in His ways
Believe in Him and He'll bless your days.
His love will lift you higher than you've ever been
As He takes away your remorse and sin!

BEYOND THE SUNSET

Beyond the sunset there's peace I know
Her awesome colors set my heart aglow
On past the magnificence of it I long to go.

I want to live above the world in that sacred heavenly place
Where I shall meet Jesus, my Savior, face to face
And all of God's children are ruled by His never-ending grace.

Beyond the sunset I see my Savior's hands outstretched to me
As he guides me daily in what He wants me to be
He offers me a taste of sweet heavenly eternity.

Beyond the sunset Dear Jesus, place your hand in mine
Make my weary heart beat in time with thine
As I inherit part of thy kingdom and make it mine.

Dear Jesus, lift me above the sunset next to your side
Where nevermore from temptation I hide
Being near you will be my utmost joy and pride.

Beyond the sunset Sweet Jesus, show me the way
I will make it my goal each and every day
And to that sunset help me, Dear Lord I pray!

BLESSINGS FROM ABOVE

Lord, show me your way
Help me to follow you each day.
Fulfill my heart by being near
Control my being and cast away my fear.

Father, God, search my heart and soul
Weed out all wickedness to make me whole.
Create a clean heart within me
Show me thy ways as I follow thee

Heavenly Father, I am so grateful for your love
Thank you for blessings that you shower from above.
I am so blest that I belong solely to you
Help me to glorify you in all that I do.

Lord, I place my trust solely in thee
I pray others will see you in me.
I am so grateful to be a child of you, the King
Your love means more to me than anything!

BLESSINGS GALORE

Trees burst out in colorful bloom
Filling the air with sweet perfume
All of nature is in tune.

Plants sprout and peep from the sod
Wild flowers in the meadows nod
Reminding me we serve an awesome God.

Birds sing joyful melodies
As they fly by and light in the trees
Butterflies dance thru the soft breeze.

Winter is over in its gloom
Soon all the pretty flowers will bloom
For summertime is coming soon.

Thank God for blessings galore
That He always keeps in store
To pour down from Heavens door!

BUTTERFLIES

Butterflies flutter thru dappled light
And are such a beautiful sight
As they feast on flowers between each flight.

Butterflies flash luminous colors of hue
They are stunning as they softly fly thru
And land giving a majestic view.

Butterflies chase each other in the air
Playing the mating game in awesome beauty rare
They leave sweet impressions and make a lovely pair.

Butterflies are so pleasing to the eye
As thru the summer breeze they fly
And disappear in the beauty of the sky!

BUTTERFLIES ARE BEAUTIFUL

Butterflies are a beautiful sight
As they flutter by and on flowers light.
They leave fond impressions on the heart
As from flower to flower they dart.

Butterflies come in many colors of hue
Many of them will amaze you.
They fly softly by without making a sound
While spreading their beauty around.

You never know butterflies are near
Until in your eyesight they suddenly appear.
Many butterflies have a touch of blue in flight
Creating a gorgeous and pleasing sight.

Butterflies are a stunning sight as they glide with ease
Casting beautiful reflections in the summer breeze.
They were created by our wondrous God above
He showers His blessings on us thru His awesome love!

BUTTERFLIES AT PLAY

While watering my flowers today
I watched two beautiful butterflies at play.
They are one of God's small creatures
And have such delicate features.

They fluttered up and down
In awesome beauty renown,
As they floated in the air serenely
Leaving pleasing reflections with me.

God creates magnificent beauty rare
He places it here for us to share.
He cast wondrous beauty in amazing ways
To brighten our view and enhance our days!

CALL ON JESUS

If you walk in darkness
And can't make it thru.
Call on Jesus for help
He's willing to rescue you.

Jesus loves you unconditionally
And waits to hear your call.
He's willing to rescue you
He'll lift you up never more to fall.

Jesus is the way, the truth and the light
When you're in deep distress,
He will protect you thru His power and might
Your life and soul He always comes to bless!

CALL UNTO JESUS

Satan rages in this world today
He yearns to take your peace of mind away.
Focus on Jesus, the Savior of your soul
His amazing love will make you whole.

When Satan throws His darts at you
Call on Jesus whose love is always true.
He'll quickly come to your rescue
Your heart and soul He stands ready to renew.

Satan will come to you in disguise
And try to deceive you with His lies.
Jesus will defeat Him; just go to Him in prayer
He always looks out for you and your welfare!

CHOOSE TO FOLLOW JESUS

Death is not the end
It will be our greatest gain,
When we meet Jesus, our Savior and friend
And move to a higher plain.

We are strangers here on earth
Seeking a place God has prepared for us with Him.
He waits to receive us and give us rebirth
We'll have everlasting eternity in His heavenly realm.

We have an eternal destination choice to make
Choose wisely the heavenly pathway to take.
Jesus is the way, the truth and the light
He alone can save you thru His power and might.

Christians are not afraid to die
But look forward to going to their home on high;
Far above where the silver clouds lie
And just beyond the beauty of the sky.

Dedicate your life to Christ this very day
Begin traveling the heavenly way.
Jesus will lead you safely there
And shelter you forever in His care!

CHRISTMAS IN HEAVEN

Christmas in heaven is more beautiful than on earth I know
Jesus is there to set all hearts and souls aglow.
Angelic voices are more melodious than here on earth
As they praise Him as their Savior and celebrate His birth.

Our loved ones in heaven are happy for eternity
In that bright land where love reigns free.
Even though our hearts are heavy and for them we grieve
If in Jesus we believe, our heavenly crown we'll soon receive.

As the face of our blessed Redeemer we see
We'll shout in acclamation and have a heavenly jubilee.
Our precious loved ones there we shall meet
And Christmas in heaven will finally be complete
As we rejoice in unison at Jesus, our Redeemers, feet!

CHRISTMAS NIGHT'S DELIGHT

Santa came by my house last night
But found no milk and cookies in sight.
Instead he found a star shining on a manger scene
Angels were bending over on hovering wing.

A tiny babe was sleeping quietly on the straw
Mary, His virgin mother, watched over in awe.
Santa winked in amazement at the wondrous sight
And left the presents beneath the stars guiding light.

As he pondered the holiness of this night
He rejoiced at the beauty in joyful delight.
He kneeled beneath the awesome show
Then got up and left with not even a ho, ho, ho!

CHRISTMAS TIME

Christmas is a glorious time of love
It's when God sent His Son, Jesus to earth from heaven above
No greater gift could we ever receive or dream of.

He was King of all even though not born in splendor
Unto to this world of sinners' great joy he did render
Praise God, His Father, as His majestic sender.

Joseph, his father and Mary, His virgin mother, could find no place to stay
Baby Jesus was born in a stable in a manger bed filled with hay
He had no pillow where His sweet head could lay.

Angels on high sang out in acclamation of His birth
Peace and good will had been sent by God to earth
Jesus would fill hearts with joy and great mirth.

Within that tiny body of baby Jesus was Salvation's plan
He taught us much while living His earthly life's span
Yet He would freely give His life to save His fellowman.

Though sinless and pure as could be
He died on the cross at Calvary
Just to sanctify and save the soul of you and me.

Our Savior was betrayed, beaten and condemned to die
He bore the cross brave and freely for sinners such as you and I
His precious blood cleansed our souls; on His grace we can rely!

CLAIM JESUS AS YOUR OWN

Claim Jesus as your Savior and Lord
Eternal Salvation is your reward.
God has the key to open your heart
So let your prayers to Him start.

God knows our heart and is quick to understand
Reach out to Him and grasp His hand.
His blessings are yours to receive
Just trust Him and on Him believe.

Jesus waits for you this very day
Accept Him and follow His way.
He'll take up residence in the heart of you
And give divine guidance thru His love so true!

DELIVERED FROM DARKNESS

God delivered us from darkness
To His blessed kingdom of light.
He sent His Son, Jesus, to the cross
To save us since we are precious in His sight.

Our sins were cleansed by Jesus' healing blood
They were nailed to the cross with Him at Calvary.
He loved us more than anyone should
His wonder working power set us free.

Jesus was betrayed, beaten and denied
Cruel was the death He suffered and died.
He was buried in a tomb that couldn't hold Him
He arose from the dead to ascend to the Heavenly realm.

Jesus sits at God's throne by His right hand
In heaven's majestic and beautiful celestial land.
He constantly looks out for our welfare
And intervenes with God, His Father, for our sins there!

DRAW ME NEARER TO THEE

Lord I'll never fear
As long as you draw me near
To ease my heartaches and my burdens bear.

Lord, I am nothing without you
Dark clouds gather and block my view
And I don't know what to do.

Nearer to you I long to be
Wrapped in your arms lovingly
My heart soars wild and free.

Lord, you are my sunshine
Lighting this path of mine
I treasure your grace and power divine.

Lord, your love amazes me
Over sin and shame, you gave me victory
My song shall forever be, draw me ever nearer to thee!

FAITH

Through faith in God we resist temptation
In our life He gives total transformation.
Faith leads us to cling tightly to Him
And trust Him to lead us to the heavenly realm.

Ask God to increase your faith right now
Your heart with His love He will endow.
God can and will accomplish great things through you
Trust Him and nothing will impossible for you to do.

Faith in God will cleanse your soul deep within
Believe in Him as He takes away all your sin.
Faith comes from hearing and studying His word
Trust Him and your soul with His armor He will gird.

Develop your faith and God will bless you
As you exercise faith, your heart and soul He'll renew.
Hold tight and cling to Jesus' nail scarred hand
Have faith in Him and follow His command!

FLOWERS LIFT OUR SPIRIT HIGH

There's nothing more beautiful than flowers
That God grows through His awesome powers.
They lift our hopes and spirits high
But they soon fade away and die.

However, through God's love and grace
He grows more beautiful ones in their place.
Praise Him for His amazing love
He's our majestic creator in heaven above!

FOLLOW JESUS

Follow Jesus and your life will change
Your priorities He will rearrange.
He will bring good out of all you do
Let others see Jesus in you.

Open your eyes to see others thru love
Keep your heart and mind focused on God above.
Reach out to others and impact lives for eternity
Spread salvations message to all you see.

Lay-up treasures for yourself in paradise
Strive to reach heaven where the soul never dies.
Make time for your fellowman and look out for their welfare
Live with a heart of gratitude and be ever ready to share.

Follow Jesus and hold tight to His nail scarred hand
He will guide you safely across this land.
Keep Him foremost in your heart and soul
His amazing grace and love will make you whole!

GIVE GOD CONTROL

God reaches down from above
He consoles us through His love.
When we struggle in life and think all is at loss
He makes a bridge for us to cross.

God comes into our life to bless
He embraces us in His loving caress.
He gives divine guidance to all His fellowman
And for our life He has a perfect plan.

God sees and knows everything we do
He stands available to come to our rescue.
We must give Him control of our heart and soul
And His amazing love will make us whole!

GLORIFY GOD

Reflect on God's mighty acts
And the miracles He performed while on earth.
His amazing love has awesome impacts
He gave His Son, Jesus, to give us rebirth.

When in life you think something is missing
Worship God and receive a blessing.
His powerful deeds can still be seen
If on His promises we lean.

Our God is majestic and superior above all
He stands ready to rescue you when you call.
Praise and glorify Him with all your heart and soul
His amazing grace and mercy will make you whole.

Thank the Lord that you belong to Him
He will light your path when dark and dim.
Worship Him in beautiful song
Glorify Him the whole day long!

GOD CALLS US ALL

IN MEMORY OF MY SISTER SHIRLEY B. KNEECE

Look towards the sky at night
To see the stars shining bright
And be assured Shirley is all right
She's in the care of Jesus who is the light!

Life is like a vapor we all know
But when God calls, it's our time to go
There's no eternity on this earth below
The spirit goes to be with Jesus who loves us so!

We will treasure memories Shirley left behind
They shall live forever in our heart and mind
She loved everyone she met and was good and kind
She has received her crown of gold silver lined!

Someday soon God will call us too
Far beyond the clouds and skies of blue
He waits patiently our body to renew
Just believe in Him and you'll make it through!

With a loving family Shirley was blest
Now she's gone to Heaven for eternal rest
She didn't want to leave but God knows what's best
She is in the arms of Jesus never more to be stressed!

She would not want us to grieve
But walk the walk with Jesus and on Him believe
Rich are the blessings we shall receive
If we walk with Him and to His precious promises cleave!

GOD CAN CHANGE YOU

Seek God's power and might
He will help you win Satan's fight.
When all your strength is gone
His love will carry you on.

You can do all things through Him
His amazing grace your heart will overwhelm.
He will fill your empty cup to the brim
And change your life that is dark and grim.

Jesus is the great and mighty Master of Divinity.
Redeemed through Him you can forever be.
He will never forsake you and stands ready to forgive
Just accept Jesus in your heart to forever live!

GOD CARRIES US ON

God's love and care are gifts we own
We never have to walk alone
His love will carry us on.

He aids us when in stress
Believe in Him and never second guess
His strength and power comes to bless.

We are a part of God's plan
He reaches out to all fellowman
Raining down rich blessings time and time again.

When our wrongs to others we can't erase
God provides us with His amazing grace
To help us resolve them and save face!

GOD EXCELS IN MERCY AND GRACE

God doesn't owe us anything
Yet, He gives us everything.
He lends mercy and grace that shall endure forever
He binds us in chords of love that no one can sever.

Our Father's works are majestic all across this land
Everywhere we look we see the touch of His hand.
He sends us bountiful blessings each day
And guides our steps to keep us from going astray.

As Lord of all He excels in mercy and grace
And protects us as thru life we frantically race.
His divine guidance serves us well
He's our Savior who can rescue us from hell!

GOD FILLS MY SOUL WITH JOYFUL GLEE

I bow down in humble praise
As my voice to God I raise.
My soul rejoices deep within
Thanking Him for bearing my sin.

I freely give unto Him my all
That ever was or may come to be.
I'm so glad He hears my call
He stands ever ready to bless me.

God holds me near to His heart
To console me as my teardrops start.
He fills my soul with joyful glee
As He makes me what He wants me to be!

GOD HOLDS US IN HIS LOVING CARESS

God does not take away our pain
But He shares it time and time again
Our tears and pain are His tears and pain.

When we cry, God cries
He sees teardrops as they flood our eyes
He grieves with us and understands more than we realize.

Never doubt God for He lingers near
We're His children and unto Him we are dear
He stands ready to take away our fear.

God will never abandon us in times of stress
He holds us near in His loving caress
Prompting us to move forward and onward press!

GOD IS AWESOME IN HIS POWERS

When I behold the golden sunset
Or see the ocean's waves break,
It creates memories I'll never forget
As I ponder beauty my God doth make.

Dear God I am constantly reminded of your beauty
I am so thankful for your majesty;
Everywhere I look great wonders I see
That you graciously bestow on me.

Lord, I praise you as King of all Kings
And rejoice in the joy your love brings;
You're the reason my heart joyfully sings
My love for you surpasses all things.

Heavenly Father, I'm so thankful for the cross of Calvary
And the gift of eternal life that you give free.
You're awesome in your wonder working power
You will always be my strong and mighty tower!

GOD IS FAITHFUL AND JUST

Mighty and holy is our Lord
He is to be forever adored.
Lift up your voice to Him in praise
He is your Redeemer now and always.

Our gracious and merciful Lord lends His love
He rains down blessings from Heaven above.
Bountiful treasures come from His hand
And He has our entire life planned.

The Lord is our strength and power
He's our solid rock and mighty tower.
Faithful and just He shall forever be
He died on the cross to give us salvation free!

GOD IS MAJESTIC

Believe and trust in God today
He'll light your path never more to stray
All you have to do is lift your heart to Him and pray.

Glorify Him and give Him complete control
His amazing love will make you whole
He comforts you when heartaches take their toll.

God is majestic in His wonder working ways
He us worthy of your admiration and praise
With love He controls your life daily in every phase.

As Lord of all He shelters you through His love
Rich blessings He rains down on you from above
More bountiful than you have ever dreamed of!

GOD IS OUR FATHER

God is our Father whom we belong to
He forgives our iniquity our life to renew.
He's an awesome God to serve
Who gives us more than we deserve.

God's grace is greater than all our sin
He can heal our soul deep within.
His Holy Spirit enters our heart and mind
And great joy and peace we find.

The gift of life to us God doth freely give
So our souls may eternally live.
There's none other like Him and shall never be
He delights in lending His mercy and grace free!

GOD IS OUR SHINING STAR

God puts us through trials at times
To let us know we can't handle things on our own.
Yet, He stands ready for us to call on
So He can help us and we won't be alone.

Our God is awesome in His ways
Through His amazing love He blesses our days.
All we have to do is believe and trust Him
And He will lighten our days that are dark and grim.

Never underestimate God's divine love and power
Rich are the blessings on us He doth shower.
He watches over us no matter where we are
And shall always be our bright and shining star!

GOD LENDS HIS LOVE

God desires that we share His word
With all others who have not heard.
It should overflow in kindness to all we meet
And have an eternal effect making life sweet.

God can transform our heart, soul and mind
Seek Him individually and true peace you'll find.
He will reset your purpose and direct you toward eternity
From all sin and shame, He will set your troubled soul free.

God wants us to come boldly to His throne of grace
He delights in administering to all who seek His face.
We can receive forgiveness through His awesome love
Great and mighty blessings He sends to us from above.

God knows and understands we are weak and need Him
He stands ready to fill our empty cup to the brim.
He waits patiently to hear us when we call
So He can lend His love to help us stand tall!

GOD LOOKS OUT FOR YOU

God, The Great I Am, created you
And has a divine purpose for you too
He knows everything that you do.

God watches over you night and day
He hears every prayer that you pray
He gives salvation free right away.

God's grace and love is free for all
He patiently waits to hear your call
So He can lift you up should you fall.

God sees you as thru life you race
He yearns to wrap you within His embrace
Just to share His awesome love and grace!

GOD LOVES YOU

God loves you more than words can tell
His love always serves you well.
Every teardrop that you shed He sees
With love He dries them away with ease.

Moment by moment He watches out for you
He knows and sees all that you do.
He feels your pain and hears your every prayer
And keeps you sheltered in His care.

God loves you more than you'll ever know
And goes with you everywhere you go.
Never will He leave you or forsake you
In times of trouble He'll help you make it thru!

GOD OF LOVE

God above, God of light
Master who controls day and night,
Precious Jesus, who died for you and me
Blessed Redeemer, you have set us free.

God of mercy, God of love
God who reigns in Heaven above,
Lord over earth and all therein
Ruler of mankind, who is conqueror of sin.

God of healing, God of grace
Savior of the entire human race,
Prince of Peace, King of all Kings
Controller and creator of all things.

Christ our Savior, Holy One
Father, the Holy Spirit, Jesus, the Son,
Shelter us within thy embrace
We long to see the beauty of your face!

GOD RESCUES US

God rescued me from deep dark stress
And filled my soul with His righteousness
Oh' what joy to feel His sweet caress
I no longer walk in darkness.

God also will give you the stamina that you need
Just invite Him into your heart and let Him lead.
He will rescue you from your sinfulness
And your heart and soul He will bless.

God offers peace to your sinful soul
His amazing love will make you whole.
Trust and believe in Him right away
He stands ready to change your darkest night to day!

GOD SENDS ANGELS

God's angels come to us
With healing rays and wings unfurled,
To support and protect us
From troubles and turmoil in this world.

Angels are always kind and true
They chase away troubles when we're blue.
Our strength and courage they renew
As they lend a helping hand in all we do.

God commands His angels from above
To share His sweet unselfish love.
They linger forever near
To cast away our heartache and fear.

God keeps angels standing close by
So when we're in distress they'll hear our cry.
Praise God for loving us so much
That He sends angels our lives to touch!

GOD SENDS THE RAINBOW

When the storm is over
And the lightening fades,
The beautiful rainbow appears
In colors of hue and translucent shades.

It's a promise from God above
To show His infinite and bountiful love.
It shines brightly for the entire world to see
Displaying His power and majesty!

GOD SENT ME AN ANGEL

An angel is hovering above
God sent him on wings of love,
To administer just to me
For He knew I needed him you see.

He floated softly down
And surrounded me with love renown.
He came to walk close by my side
So he could be my comfort and guide.

God commanded him to protect me from all harm
And wrap me in his arms safe and warm.
He is to be my guardian angel from now on
So I will never have to walk alone.

I feel his love all around
I know he will keep me safe and sound.
God knew exactly what I needed
So thru His mercy and love He interceded!

GOD SHINES HIS LOVE LIGHT

When your way becomes too dark to see
And your life is blocked with adversity,
When no one else seems to care
Take it to the Lord in prayer.

If you can't find the way to go
Jesus will light your way; this I know.
He'll renew your faith; believe in Him
His love your heart and soul will overwhelm.

When despair comes on the darkest night
God stands ready to give His guiding light.
He'll take away your aching pain
And revive your trembling soul again.

Sometimes no matter what you do
Dark clouds will block your view.
Yet God will shine His love light on you
To assure that you, His child, will make it thru!

GOD TOUCHED ME

I talked with God just today
Down in the wildwood where I used to play
As I knelt down on my knees to pray.

I met with Him in this enchanted place
With a desire to see Him face to face
And He blessed me through His grace.

God reached down and touched me on my sleeve
Told me if only in Him I would believe
Rich blessings would be mine to receive.

He gently placed His hand in mine
Filling my heart with love genuine
Then He made me a branch of Him, the vine.

God lifted my burdens and cast away my shame
Within my heart He lit a burning flame
And I knew my life would never be the same!

GOD'S GIFTS

God gives beautiful sunsets
And stars above the sky to light.
He leaves impressions the mind never forgets
And changes the day to night.

He lights the paths you take
And walks close by your side.
He watches over you when sleeping and awake
And listens as in Him you confide.

He sends bountiful blessings night and day
And hears every prayer that you pray.
He commands angels to watch over you
And intervene in your life if needed to.

He offers unconditional love
In ways you've never thought of.
His Son, Jesus, died your soul to save
And free you from being Satan's slave.

You are Gods child and shall forever be
Greater still He offers you eternity
You'll sing and shout the victory
As you reign in His heavenly home eternally!

GOD'S GRACE

God's grace, how can it be
His amazing grace has redeemed me?
I was lost and sinking deep in sin
Until He shined His grace to my life within.

His only Son, Jesus, bore the cross
So I would not be forever lost.
He shed His precious blood
And cleansed my sin with the flood.

I'm so thankful Jesus paid the price I owe
Just because He loved me so.
His amazing love set my soul free
From sin and shame, He won my victory!

GOD'S HANDS

As you travel through this life
You will face much sin and strife.
God, your Savior, always looks out for you
Trust in him and He'll see you through.

God's hands reach out to heal you
And mend your heart when broke in two.
Reach out and hold tight to God's hands
He will guide you safely through these lands.

God will keep you safe from Satan's snares
For you and your soul He deeply cares.
He stands ever ready to rescue you
His amazing love is always fresh and new!

GOD'S LOVE

God sees that you are blest
He always gives you His best.
Rich blessings He sends each day
Love and goodness He passes your way.

Believe in God and you'll see
He'll touch you in His majesty.
He is always available to call on
Never will He leave you alone.

Share His love, hope and goodwill
He will make your heart quiet and still.
Just go to Him in prayer on bended knee
From sin and shame He will set you free!

GOD'S LOVE IS GENUINE

When I go to God in prayer
I never have to worry; He's always there
He stays ready to shelter me in His care.

He lets me know His love is genuine
As He works miracles in this life of mine
He shares His blessings through love divine.

Dedicate your life to Him this very day
He stands ready to take your heartaches away
And He yearns to come into your heart to stay.

God's Son, Jesus, is a beacon shining bright
Surrounding you with His love light
That leads to heaven's fair city where there is no night!

GOD'S PRESENCE

When we come into God's presence
We're standing on Holy Ground,
Within the light of His majestic love
Where scores of angels' surround.

He reaches deep into our hearts
As His loving ways He imparts.
Amazing grace to us He reveals
Our fate He forever seals.

God's presence is sacred and supreme
He has power to save and redeem.
Lift up your voices unto Him and sing
Praise Him as Savior and King!

GOD'S PROMICES

Trust and believe in me
I will set your soul free
And lead you to heavenly eternity.

Come walk close by my side
I hold my arms of love open wide
And I want to be your Master and Guide.

Never fear the dark unknown
I stay near for you to call on
So you won't have to walk alone.

Offer me prayers and seek my face
I will bless you thru my mercy and grace
And lead you to a most sacred hiding place!

GOD'S REDEEMING LOVE

God lends His mercy and grace to all
His awesome love lifts us up when we fall
It enables us to stand tall.

God created us to live for Him
He lights our way when dark and dim
His Son, Jesus, died to pave our way to heavens realm.

Jesus can renew your life and set you free
Accept his gift of love and live eternally
He proved His mercy when He died at Calvary.

Jesus paid the debt that we all owe
And set our hearts and souls aglow
So His redeeming love we would forever know!

GOD'S VOICE

There's a voice deep within my soul
That keeps my life in control.
It speaks to me when I lose hope
And gives me courage to cope.

The voice comes from God above
He shelters me in His perfect love.
I'm so thankful He speaks to me
Just to teach me His love and humility.

Lord of all, keep thy voice speaking
For it's your love I'm forever seeking.
My greatest goal is to walk close to you
And bask in your love so true.

I'm just a pilgrim passing your way
Constantly listening to what you say.
Lord, I daily seek your face
And will abide eternally in your grace!

GOD WILL DELIVER US

God's presence is ever near
His love is steadfast and clear.
He's not only in our life, but outside too
His promises are always true.

God loves us beyond measure
His holiness brings great pleasure.
His love He gives free and it is needed so
It is with us no matter where we go.

God watches over us night and day
In our struggles He clears the way.
He's faithful to deliver all who believe
Great are His blessings we receive.

God knows we need Him desperately
He knows all and can see,
The fallen world that we face
And stands ready to deliver us thru His grace!

GRACE

God's glory shines proud and true
His grace He sends to you.
It is a sacred gift from Him above
Given through the death of His Son in love.

Grace is what we stand on today
With power to take all guilt away.
When we are weak, it makes us strong
And sustains us our entire life long.

We cannot be saved apart from grace
It lights our heart as through life we race.
It's everything we are or ever will be
Grace sets the burdened heart free.

God's grace lifts us to our highest peak
It is free when God's will we seek.
Trust in God and let Him have His way
He will flood your soul with His grace today!

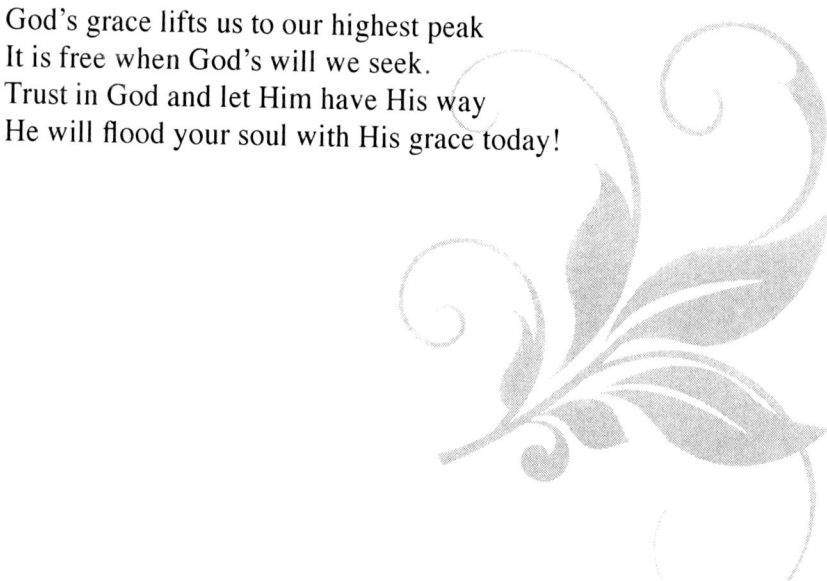

GRACE AND MERCY

God's grace and mercy excels
Our hearts with love it swells.
With Him as our Master and guide
There's no way we will backslide.

God gifted us with His Son
Victory over sin and shame He won,
When He shed His blood at Calvary
To ransom the souls of you and me.

God's grace and mercy last throughout eternity
Jesus, His Son, offers eternal life free.
Reach out now and grasp His nail scared hand
He will lead you safely to Heavens land!

GRIEF IS ONLY TEMPORARY

Lord, we're in deep grief
And ask you for sweet relief.
Our loved one in death slipped away
Turning our skies to a somber gray.

We know for each of us you have a plan
That escapes no woman or man.
Yet we fail to understand why
Our loved ones have to die.

It leaves us lonesome and heartbroken too
Although we know we must trust in you;
And lift our hearts to you above
So we may believe in your eternal love.

Someday soon our earthly journey will be over too
And our spirit will soar to meet you,
Far beyond the sky just beyond the setting sun
Then we'll be reunited with our loved one.

We'll have a heavenly jubilee
Down by the beautiful crystal sea.
We'll sing and shout the victory
Thanking you, Lord of all, for salvation free!

HEAL OUR NATION LORD

Lord we need you desperately
Fast we are losing our liberty.
We fully trust in your power
Rich blessings on us to shower.

Our nation has turned away from you
In the many wicked things they do.
We all are sinners by choice
Yet we still need to heed your voice.

Lord, just intervene in our nation today
Take all hate, hurt and racism away.
Blend us in unity with our fellowman
Help us to share salvations plan.

Lord, we have no hope other than you
Bless our nation; make us proud and true.
Reach down with thy almighty hand
And heal our troubled sin sick land!

HEARLD ANGELS ARE SINGING

Christmas bells are ringing
Listen and you will hear them.
Herald angels are singing
Of a new born babe and praising Him.

God knew we needed a Savior
So He sent His Son, Jesus, to earth,
To help us reach heaven's door
Through salvation's plan and rebirth.

Although Jesus had no sin
He chose to die for you and me,
So a new life we could begin
And our soul would forever ransomed be.

He freely bore the cross at Calvary
And shed His precious blood,
In atonement for our iniquity
Our sins were washed away with the great flood.

Believe in Him and follow His ways
He will cleanse your heart and soul,
And set your entire being ablaze
His amazing grace will make you whole!

HEAVEN'S LAND

There's a beautiful river that flows free
Jesus, our Savior, waits there for you and me.
Just trust in Jesus; He'll take your hand
And help you cross that river to Heaven's Land.

When finally, our Father's face we see
We will sing and shout the victory.
He will take us gently by the hand
And lead us to the Promised Land.

We'll meet our Father God of all creation
And kneel before His throne in admiration
To thank Him for our eternal salvation
As we glorify Him in heartfelt appreciation!

<u>Chorus</u>
Sweet Jesus, take my hand
Lead me to Heaven's Land
Where I'll make my final stand;
Help me cross that river flowing free
I can hardly wait your face to see
I want to worship you through eternity

I AM YOURS AND YOU ARE MINE

Thank you God for sending Jesus, your Son, to die for my sin
He died to conquer my sin so a new life I could begin
I am so grateful He touched my soul giving me peace within.

Lord, you placed all my sin on the Sacrificial Lamb
So I might become righteous and make me what I am
Now and forever there's no way Satan my soul can damn.

Jesus' blood covered my sin through His mercy and grace
And through His Majesty He gave me a sacred hiding place
Within the realm of His love as through this hectic life I race.

Loving Savior, I am proud to be called a child of thine
And thankful for your true love so genuine
Now and forever I am yours and you are mine!

I BELONG TO JESUS

I turned my life over to Jesus long ago
And His amazing love I have come to know.
With Him as my Master and Guide
There is no way I can backslide.

He guides my actions and clears the way
As I travel through life each day.
I keep Him deep within my heart
So His loving ways He can impart.

Jesus has taught me so many things
Until my soul joyfully sings.
He is the great and mighty I Am
The Son of God and the Sacrificial Lamb.

Jesus directs me toward His heavenly realm
He lights my path when dark and dim.
I belong to Jesus and Jesus belongs to me
He shall be mine throughout eternity!

I CAN ONLY IMAGINE

I can only imagine
Entering Heaven's pearly gates,
And meeting Jesus, my Savior
In that celestial land where He waits.

I can only imagine
How blissful it will be,
As I join my Redeemer
Who gave His life, His all for me.

I can only imagine
Walking with Jesus hand in hand,
Just to view the majestic treasures
Of rubies and diamonds in that fair land.

I can only imagine
Treading on streets of purest gold,
And the beautiful sights
My eyes will behold.

I can only imagine
Strolling down beside the crystal sea
To sing with the angels in unity
As I join in with the heavenly jubilee.

I can only imagine
Being eternally in God's care
Where peace and joy pervade the air
And there's not a storm cloud anywhere.

I can only imagine
A perfect haven with no night,

Where love reigns free
And Jesus is the light.

I can only imagine
Joy that will flood my soul,
When I meet my loved ones
And we let the hallelujahs roll.

I can only imagine
Kneeling at the holy throne,
And praising the Three In One
Throughout eternity from now on!

I CLAIM JESUS AS MY OWN

My soul sings to Jesus in His greatness
I praise Him in His righteousness.
I give thanks to Him and glorify His name
For His holiness and the price He paid for my shame.

I rejoice in knowing I can claim Jesus as my own
He will never leave me and is the greatest friend I've known.
When I'm heavy laden, I find rest in His care
Gracious and merciful is He; my burdens He will bear.

Great is my Father's faithfulness in watching over me each day
I am so grateful to Him for blessings He sends my way.
He doesn't owe me anything; yet He gives me everything
His love is forever mine and unto Him I shall forever cling!

I CHERISH MY REDEEMERS LOVE

My Lord and Savior, I cherish your love
I'll always glorify your divine intervention from above
When I'm tempest tossed and others push and shove
Your spirit descends on me like a beautiful dove.

When darkness covers my soul to blind my sight
And I refuse to move forward and lose the will to fight
Sweet Jesus, your countenance shines bright
My dark and dreary path it will light.

My Redeemer, I praise your holy name
You're the Lamb of God who took all blame
Your love has forever lit a flame
It cleansed me from all sin and shame.

Precious Jesus, I'll forever worship you
I know your love is forever true
You gave me a chance to start life anew
And healed my spirit that was broke in two!

I DREAMED OF HEAVEN

Last night I dreamed I went to Heaven
And walked on the streets of pure gold;
The city was filled with beauty rare
And so breathtaking to behold.

I saw hosts of angels everywhere
I could feel God's presence near.
Suddenly I saw Him on His throne
And experienced joy I've never known.

Jesus, my Savior, was there with Him too
Intervening for sins my heart and soul to renew.
Songs of heavenly hosts led me in a door
Where angels bid me welcome forever more.

When I awoke to find
I'd only traveled there in my mind,
I prayed for God to search my soul
And cast my iniquity away to make me whole!

IF I COULD NEVER PRAY

Where would I be
If unto God, I could never pray?
And what would happen to me
If He didn't guide my way?

What would I do
If God's light did not shine;
To illuminate my path and brighten my view
Lost would be this soul of mine.

I wouldn't be able to make it on my own
My heart would be heavy with all joy gone.
I couldn't sing a sweet, sweet song
My faith and courage wouldn't be strong.

I'd have no reason for living
Without the blessings He keeps giving.
If I could never pray, my heart would never sing
Praises to God, my Savior, Lord and King!

IF ONLY

If only you'll take God's hand
And follow Him at His command
He will carry you safely across this land.

If only you'll believe in Him
He'll brighten your path that is dim
And fill your empty cup to the brim.

If only you'll reach out to mankind
And help them our Savior find
God will give you peace of mind.

If only you will kneel and pray
Jesus will take your sins away
And direct you the heavenly way!

IN CHRIST I STAND

In Christ I stand; I am His and He is mine
He cleansed my soul through His power divine.
His love made me what I ought to be
His grace took away my sin and set me free.

He freed my soul and ransomed me
Over sin and shame, He gave me victory.
Satan can never pluck me from His hand
He's mine forever; in Christ I'll always stand.

No one can deter me from believing in Him
He'll light my path when my vision grows dim.
I'll live for only Him and take up His command
Christ claimed me as His and in His love I'll forever stand!

I NEED YOU LORD

Lord, when dark shadows fall
And block my sight,
Stay close beside me
Lend thy guiding light.

I long to be close beside thee
And bask in your grace and majesty.
Your love calms me as no one else can
Stay ever near me; I'll need you time and time again.

Lord there is no one like you
Your love is forever loyal and true.
You, my Redeemer, died in my place
And shed thy atoning blood to save me through grace!

I PRAISE YOU LORD

I praise you Lord for your love and grace
And long to enter thy most sacred hiding place.
I worship you and give glory to your precious name
Through grace you took away my iniquity and shame.

Lord, you displayed love in the first degree
Just to redeem and ransom me eternally,
When you shed your healing blood to pay the price for my sin
So I could be born again and have peace within.

Oh' Precious Savior, wrap me in the loving arms of thee
My greatest desire is to be yours throughout eternity.
You are my hearts song and life line
I'm so glad to claim you as mine!

I SEEK AFTER YOU LORD

Lord, deep within my heart
I seek solely after you.
Cleanse my soul through and through
As thy own loving ways you impart.

Give my spirit a heavenly desire
Within my life light a spiritual fire.
Drive thy truths deep within my soul
Through mercy and grace make me whole.

Lord, I rest my hope on only thee
Your atoning blood gave new life to me.
Precious Lamb of God you set me free
Now I shall forever ransomed be.

Help me to be good and kind
Heal me body soul and mind.
Impart your grace in all that I do
May my acts of love emulate you?

Lord, just show me your will and way
Hold me close never more to stray.
Search my heart; weed out my sinful ways
I'll exalt you and give you highest praise!

I SING UNTO MY KING

Precious Jesus, who died for me
To give me salvation and sweet eternity;
You are perfection in your sovereignty
And I know you shall forever be.

Blessed Savior, who reigns on high
I rejoice in knowing you are standing by,
To deliver me when you hear my cry
You'll gather me in your arms to hold me nigh.

Lord of all, joyfully unto you I sing
To glorify you and praise you as my King.
Great peace into my life you bring
Your amazing love means more than anything.

Lamb of God, I'll forever worship you
And praise you, my Redeemer, whose love is true.
I can never thank you for all that you do
So I'll exalt you my entire life through!

I WANT TO FOLLOW YOU LORD

Lord, place your hand on my trembling brow
Bathe me in the light of your love just now.

Cleanse my heart through thy power divine
Make my soul with thy majestic glory shine.

Walk close beside me in this weary troubled world
Protect me from Satan's darts constantly hurled.

Give me the grace and wisdom that I need
To follow in your footsteps as you lead!

I WANT TO KNEEL AT GOD'S THRONE

What an awesome day it will be
When God's blessed face I see
I'll sing and shout in victory!

In admiration I'll kneel at God's throne
I'll worship Him from that day on
In Heaven's land where there's no sin to condone.

I'll thank God for His redeeming grace
And His amazing love He allowed me to embrace
That brought me to Heavens wondrous place.

I'll adore Him and give Him highest praise
For His winsome love and healing rays
That blessed my life in so many ways!

I WANT TO SEE GOD

I want to see God and look upon his face
I want to enter His heavenly realm.
I want to feast upon His mercy and grace
I want to walk hand in hand with Him.

I want to kneel before God's throne
And praise Him in His deity from now on.
I want to tread heaven's streets of gold
And peruse the many treasures untold.

I want to serve God throughout eternity
And thank Him for the blessings He rained on me.
I want to sing with the angel band
As I make my great and final stand.

I want to glorify Jesus for giving salvation free
And praise Him for loving a sinner like me.
I want to join in with the heavenly jubilee
And serenade Jesus, my Savior, down by the crystal sea!

I WANT TO SEE JESUS

I want to see Jesus in His majesty
I'll worship Him forever in His deity.
I long to be with Him where He waits
Just inside heavens gates.

I want to see Jesus, the Great I am
He's the Master of Divinity; the Sacrificial Lamb.
He pardoned my sins on the cross at Calvary
He shed His atoning blood for me.

I want to see Jesus and hear the angels sing
Praises to Him our almighty King.
My spirit longs to meet Him face to face
I want to be immersed in His love and grace!

I WILL FOLLOW YOU LORD

Thank you Lord for giving me a new day
May I use it for your glory I humbly pray?
Walk close beside me wherever I go
Lead me where thy majestic healing waters flow.

I'm just a sinner seeking to do your will
Make my trembling heart quiet and still.
I'll follow in thy footsteps wherever you lead
Give me your grace and mercy that I sorely need.

Lord, cleanse my heart and purify my soul
I trust you and give you complete control.
You are the truth, the light and the way
Give me courage to follow you never more to stray!

I WILL GLADLY FOLLOW JESUS

My heart was heavy and filled with strife
I needed divine guidance in my life.
Suddenly I heard my Savior whisper to me
"Come my child; I'll lead you to eternity."

"I will take all your sin and guilt away
Just to brighten your life's pathway.
Trust me and follow my command
I will lead you to Heaven's fair land."

Dear Jesus, I will gladly follow you
And do the things you would have me to.
Take this broken spirit of mine
And bind it closely to thy heart divine!

I WILL NEVER WALK ALONE

Jesus resides deep within my soul
He intervenes when heartaches take a toll.
He's my Savior, Lord and the Sacrificial Lamb
He is God's own Son and the Great I Am.

Jesus means more to me than earthly things
Great is the joy to my life He brings.
The beauty of His amazing love shall forever be
And I know beyond a doubt that He loves me.

Jesus holds my hand as thru life I go
To quicken my step when I'm tired and slow.
He resolves my troubles until I have none
And will hold my hand until life is done.

Jesus will never leave or forsake me
He is mine forever throughout eternity.
He is the greatest friend I have ever known
With Him by my side I will never walk alone!

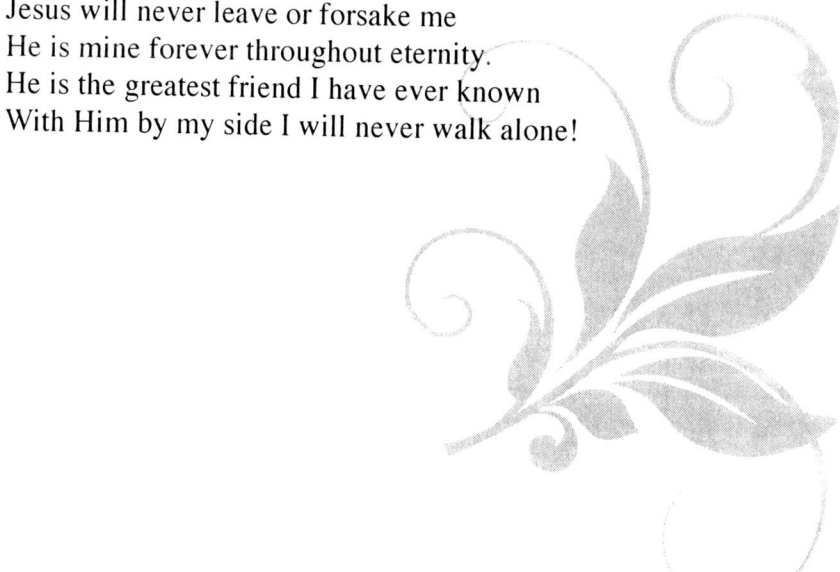

JESUS AND ME

Lost forever my soul would be
If not for the relationship of Jesus and me.
He shined His love light to my soul within
And cast out all my remorse and sin.

Jesus lifted me from the depths of hell
Through His love that serves me so well.
He is my Master, Savior and the Great I Am
He's God's own Son who is the Sacrificial Lamb.

Life would be empty if not for Jesus and me
His amazing grace and love gave me victory.
I'll glorify His name throughout eternity
And walk within His light until His face I see!

JESUS ASSURES THAT YOU'RE BLEST

Place your worries in Jesus' hands
He stands ready to give healing rest.
Cast your cares on Him and follow His commands
He will lift you up and assure that you're blest.

Our Lord and Savior has gracious and righteous ways
He is our shield and strong and mighty tower.
He loves you, so be still and give Him highest praise
When heavy laden, He will rescue you thru His power.

The Lord is good; give thanks to Him above
His mercy and grace endures forever.
Grace that is greater than all sin is portrayed thru His love
He binds us to Him with cords of love that no one can sever.

Lift Jesus' name high; His love is forever true
Let the world know exactly how you stand.
Glorify Him above all in what you say and do
Praise Him all across this land!

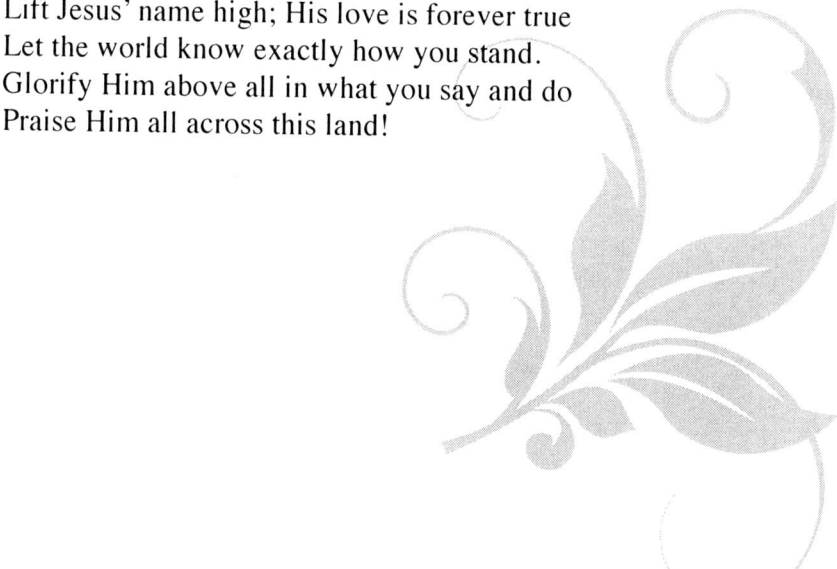

JESUS' AWESOME LOVE

Jesus knew my life was grim
So He drew me close to Him
My heart and soul to overwhelm.

Jesus and only Jesus holds the key
To redeem and sanctify me
From sin and shame, He set me free.

Jesus is the alpha and omega, Gods own Son
His amazing love out shines the sun
Victory over death and the grave He won.

Jesus picked me up when tempest tossed
To assure I would not be forever lost
He rescued me from sin at a high cost.

Jesus gave His life at Calvary
Just to save sinners like me
His awesome redeeming love shall forever be!

JESUS CAN MAKE YOU WHOLE

If you're troubled in your soul
And want to be made whole,
Take Jesus' outstretched hand
And follow His command.

He will lead you in paths of righteousness
Through His awesome love your life He will bless.
He'll light your path where ever you go
For you are His child that He loves so.

Jesus is your Savior who died on the cross for you
He took away your sin your heart and soul to renew.
Keep Him foremost in your life
His amazing grace will take away your sin and strife!

JESUS DIED FOR OUR SINS

Jesus bore the cross at Calvary
To take our sins away and offer eternal victory
Through His amazing grace and mercy.

Jesus knew our sins He could erase
So He poured out His life's blood through His grace
And freely chose to die for the human race.

God in His glory sent His Son, Jesus, to us as a gift
To be a healing balm to us and our spirits lift
Near to His heart so into sin we would not drift.

God knew we needed a solid rock to stand upon
So He sent perfection in Jesus, His only Son
Who knew victory over sin could be won.

We needed a Savior our soul to save
And a Redeemer who our path to Heaven could pave
So unto Satan we would not be forever a slave!

JESUS DRAWS YOU CLOSE TO HIM

Jesus, the Son of God, died on the cross
He gave salvation so you wouldn't be lost.
When His holy spirit enters into your heart and soul
His amazing love will make you whole.

First and foremost, you must trust in Him
He stands available to light your path that is dim.
Jesus is the solid rock on which you can stand
Lay aside worldly things and follow His command.

All you have to do is believe and grasp His hand
He can rescue you from perils and sinking sand.
He shall take residence in your heart from now on
Your life will change; all heartache and fear will be gone.

Jesus will draw you close to him
And fill your empty cup to the brim.
He, your Savior, yearns to rescue you
Trust Him your heart and soul to renew!

JESUS GIVES ETERNAL REST

Jesus is the cornerstone of our life
He takes away all sin and strife.
When in life dark shadows fall
He's always there to help us stand tall.

As temptations hidden snares
Take us unawares,
He shows He cares
As our heartaches He bears.

If you wonder, why the test
Lean on Jesus who gives eternal rest.
Soon our troubles on earth will cease
And we'll dwell with Him eternally in peace.

Jesus who died on Calvary's cross
To assure we would not be lost,
Intervenes at God, His Fathers, right hand
To pave our way to Heavens land!

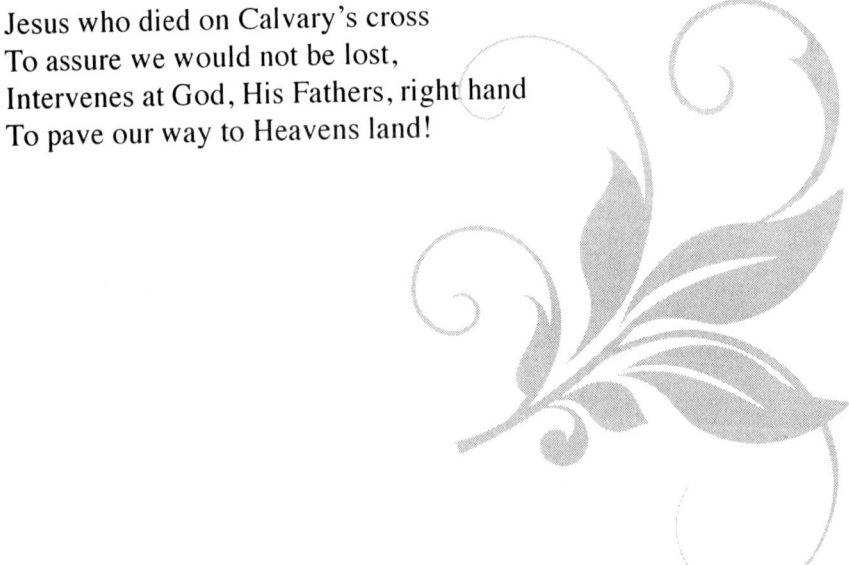

JESUS GIVES SALVATION AND ETERNAL LIFE

As we follow Jesus to the cross He bore
And look upon the crown of thorns He wore,
We think of how He was ridiculed and betrayed
And the price for our sins He paid.

Jesus opened doors that were never opened before
He gives salvation and eternal life forever more.
All we have to do is trust and believe in Him
And His amazing love our heart and soul will overwhelm!

JESUS' GLORY AND GRACE

Did you know Jesus dearly loves you?
And can mend your heart that is broke in two
His love is forever powerful and true.

He stands ready listening for your call
So He can help you thru it all
As your Savior, He will pick you up if you fall.

Trust His word and believe in Him
He will fill your empty cup to the brim
And light your pathway that is dim.

Jesus is your Savior and the Great I Am
Gods own Son and the Sacrificial Lamb
He'll save you from Satan's power to damn.

All of His children to Him are dear
Just call on Him; He will hear
And cast away your doubt and fear.

Jesus will never forsake you nor leave you alone
He's the greatest protector and friend ever known
His love will sustain you until all heartaches are gone.

He will shelter you in His warm embrace
Your heart with anticipation will race
As you experience His glory and grace!

JESUS, GREATEST NAME I KNOW

Jesus, Jesus, greatest name I know
You're my Lord and Savior who loves me so.
There's no power greater than thy own
Your precious blood for sin did atone.

Jesus, Jesus, who hears my every prayer
And keeps me sheltered in your care,
There's no place I'd rather be
Than sheltered in the arms of thee.

Jesus, precious Jesus, I sing a sweet song
And will sing it over and over from now on
Until the night is over and day has gone
Glorifying you for never leaving me alone.

Jesus, majestic Jesus, I praise you for loving me
And giving thy special gift of Salvation free.
I'll keep you locked deep within my heart and soul
And give you honor and glory for making me whole!

JESUS' HAND IN MINE

Jesus keeps His hand in mine
Just because He loves me so.
His grace and love divine
Now and forever I shall know.

Jesus' hand is constantly in mine
Each day every place I go.
My soul with His doth intertwine
And He'll never leave me I know.

As long as Jesus' hand is in mine
I'll never have to walk alone.
He assures me of His love genuine
And is the greatest friend I've ever known!

JESUS IS ALWAYS NEAR

If your heart is breaking
And you can't ease the aching,
Call on Jesus; He's always near
He will take away all heartache and fear.

When trials come and no one seems to care
Jesus, our Savior, will look out for your welfare.
He can cast all of your burdens away
And turn your darkest night to day.

Simply put your trust in Him
He will fill your life that is grim,
With countless blessings from above
And rain down His sweet unselfish love.

Jesus will never let you down
He'll fill your life with joy renown,
And blanket you safely in His care
For eternity thru His love and grace so rare!

JESUS IS EASY TO FIND

Look for Jesus, He is always easy to find
He wants to control your heart and mind
What's more He offers you a mansion silver lined.

Just fall down on your knees and pray
He, your Redeemer, will take your sin away
And enfold you in His love never more to stray.

Open your heart and let His love shine in
He will cleanse your soul deep within
And make you happier than you've ever been.

Jesus is the great and mighty anointed one
His majesty and glory outshines the sun
Trust Him; He'll take you to heaven when life is done!

JESUS IS IN CONTROL

My soul was black with sin
Until Jesus, my Savior, came in
He gave me peace deep within.

Jesus took all my pain and sorrow away
He planted my feet on higher ground to stay
He changed my darkest night to day.

Jesus knew exactly what I needed
So, in my life He quickly interceded
He offered His mercy and love as He pleaded.

Jesus shined His love light in my soul
His amazing grace made me whole
Now and forever in my life He maintains control!

JESUS IS KING OF ALL KINGS

Lord God, thank you for this wondrous season
And the blissful joy of knowing Jesus, your Son, is the reason.
You sent Him to earth, as a gift of love, to live among man
Within His tiny body lay salvation's plan.

Jesus ministered for many years here on earth
He eventually died on a cross at Calvary to prove His worth.
Although we were sinful and unworthy as could be
He shed His precious blood and died for you and me.

Our sins were covered with His bloods healing flow
Our hearts were washed as white as snow.
Although He was pure and sinless He had to die
Just to give us a chance to meet Him in heaven by and by.

All we have to do is simply trust Him and on Him believe
And His gift of salvation and eternal life is ours to receive.
So lift your heart and soul to Him as it joyfully sings
Praise Jesus, the Son of God, as King of all Kings!

JESUS IS MY COMFORTER

When my heart is heavy with burdens I can't bear
I turn them over to the Lord in prayer.
He helps me to understand how to forgive
As within the majesty of His love I daily live.

Jesus, my Savior, molds my life to His will
He makes my heart quiet and still.
He wraps me safely in His loving arms
And protects me from all worldly harms.

Jesus through grace rescues me from Satan's snare
And places all my heartache in His care,
While teaching me to love others more each day
As I follow His perfect will and way.

Jesus cleanses my heart through His power divine
Until my soul with His glory doth shine.
He gives me grace and wisdom to understand
When things come into my life I haven't planned!

JESUS IS KING

The eastern star is shining bright
Oh what a glorious sight
It reminds me of Christmas night.

A tiny babe sleeps quietly on the hay
In a Bethlehem stable far away
No room in an inn could be found to stay.

Wrapped in swaddling clothes in a manager bed
With not even a pillow for His sweet head
God sent His Son, the Messiah, to earth as He said.

Glad tidings to earth He did bring
Angels on bended wing proclaim Him as king
As they praise Him and joyfully sing.

Within His tiny body lay salvation's plan
He shed His life's blood to redeem His fellowman
He gave us hope that no one else can.

His name is Jesus and He's the anointed one
Amazing grace He gives that out shines the sun
On Calvary's cross victory over our sins He won.

Believe in Him and follow His will and way
He will take all your sins away
And keep you in His care never more to stray.

He freely gave His life our soul to save
And our way to heaven pave
Praise Him in His righteousness for being bold and brave!

JESUS IS MY KING

Jesus makes my heart sing
I am so thankful He is my King.
He spreads His love around
Within my life it doth abound.

He has paved my path to eternity
Sweet is the grace He sheds on me.
I live within His shadow each day
As He guides me along life's way.

I am so grateful for blessings He sends
And His amazing love that never ends.
All praise be to Him on high
His precious name I'll forever magnify!

JESUS IS MY RIGHTEOUSNESS

Dear Jesus, I am nothing but a sinner seeking your face
I ask for your forgiveness and grace.
I know that you dearly love me
You died on the cross to set me free.

Thank you for freeing me of my sin
Your act of love gave me peace deep within.
Help me walk within thy guiding light
Protect me thru thy power and might.

Change my heart; let me run a Godly race
Give me courage for trials that I face.
Jesus, Son of God, and lover of my soul
You and you alone I will forever extol.

Dear Jesus, only you could love me so much
You bore the cross at Calvary giving a healing touch.
I have no righteousness of my own
It comes from you and you alone!

JESUS IS OUR KING

I was lost deep in sin
Jesus cleansed my soul deep within.
He as my Savior and King
Made me feel as free as a bird on wing.

My life was empty with no reason to go on
Now all my heartaches are gone.
He lifted my burdens and made me whole
I gave Him complete control.

Jesus stands ready to be your King
Great joy to your life He will bring.
His grace and love will take your guilt away
Trust and believe in Him; He'll save you today!

JESUS IS OUR SAVIOR

Our God is glorious in His divine holiness
No one can work miracles like Him.
He wraps us in His loving caress
And lights our path when dark and dim.

God sent His Son, Jesus, to us here below
To die on the cross so His redeeming grace we may know.
Jesus who had no sin took all of our blame
So we could come to God, His Father, with no shame.

Pure and spotless Lamb of God was He
Yet He chose to die to redeem you and me.
Jesus, our Savior, arose from death in victory
Trust and believe in Him; He offers eternity.

He intervenes with God, His Father, yet today
As He offers salvation free and takes our guilt away.
Accept Him as your Savior; salvation He freely gives
Rejoice in knowing that He forever lives!

JESUS IS THE ANSWER

When you are lost and all alone
There is someone you can call on.
Jesus stays available day and night
He'll rescue you and make things right.

Ask Jesus to come into your heart
His loving ways he will impart.
He'll take your heart that is broke in two
And through His grace make it like new.

Jesus knows exactly how you feel
His amazing grace and power is real.
He takes your burdens when too heavy to bear
He places them safely in His care.

When you're troubled and filled with fear
He's there beside you since He stays near.
He patiently waits for your call
So He can lift you up never more to fall!

JESUS IS THE ATONING SACRIFICE

Jesus is the atoning sacrifice for our sin
Open your heart and let His love shine in.
Come to know Him and obey His commands
Follow Him and hold tight to His nail scarred hands.

Your sins have been forgiven solely on the account of Him
He stands ready to light your path to never grow dim.
Keep the word of God within your heart to overcome temptation
Cling to Him with utmost love and complete dedication.

Be not lovers of the world for it will pass away
Follow the will of God and glorify Him night and day.
Many false prophets will come and try to lead you astray
Remain steadfast in the Lord; be careful what you do and say.

Continue in the Lord so when He appears you may be confident
We all are children of God given a chance from sin to repent.
When Jesus appears we shall be in His likeness
He laid down His life so our souls could heavenward press!

JESUS IS THE MORNING STAR

All honor and glory to God above
He sent us His Son, Jesus, to show His love.
He came from heaven to earth
To ransom our soul and give us rebirth.

Jesus is the morning star that rises in our heart
Through His Majesty He completes our inner most part.
He's our Lord and Savior who forever reigns
He can take away all of our heartaches and pains.

Jesus died on the old rugged cross at Calvary
He poured out His life's blood to ransom you and me.
He arose from the grave in total victory
Today and forever He gives us a chance to live eternally.

He ascended to heaven and sits at the right hand of God's throne
There He intercedes with Him for our sins from now on.
Like a thief in the night the Lord is coming back some day
Be on your guard so you won't be carried away.

Dedicate your life; grow in grace and knowledge of our Lord
Serve Him and trust His divine word in sweet accord.
God is light; in Him there is no darkness
Walk in His light; your heart and soul He will bless!

JESUS IS THE REASON FOR THE SEASON

Christmas is a wondrous season
Jesus is the primary reason.
God sent His Son, Jesus, long ago
His amazing love to show.

Precious was the gift God sent
Jesus spread love everywhere He went.
Yet He was betrayed and crucified.
On a cross at Calvary He died.

He died to save His fellowman
And gave hope thru salvations plan.
He changed the world more than we know
His grace and love set our paths aglow!

JESUS IS THERE FOR YOU AND ME

When we cross life's stormy sea
Jesus is always there for you and me.
As billows around us roll
He, our Master, keeps control.

Jesus is the greatest comforter ever known
He'll never forsake us or leave us alone.
He offers unconditional love rich and free
He's the Great I Am and Master of Divinity.

Jesus constantly waits to hear our call
So He can pick us up when we fall.
His amazing love will never let us down
Our heart and soul with joy He will crown.

So when trials come and you are tempest tossed
Call on Jesus; He'll bring you in when lost.
He, your Savior, will keep you safe and sound
And will assure that you are heaven bound!

JESUS KNOCKED ON MY HEARTS DOOR

Jesus knocked lightly on my hearts door
I had heard Him knocking many times before.
My wandering mind could never conceive
It was Jesus, my Savior, in whom I believe.

He asked me to have more resilience and pray
For the redemption of the less fortunate than I each day.
Quietly down on my knees I bended
Since finally His message I comprehended.

Jesus is my Precious Redeemer who keeps me in line
When things don't go right He gives me a sign.
I praise Him for loving sinners like me
I'll walk hand in hand with Him throughout eternity!

JESUS LIFTS ME UP

Jesus' love is forever genuine
I'm so glad He is a friend of mine.
His mercy is great; His grace is free
Thru His amazing love He redeemed me.

Each time I stumble and fall on my face
Jesus picks me up thru His grace.
He wipes my dirty face clean
As on His everlasting arms I lean.

Hallelujah Lord, don't ever give up on me
I need your love throughout eternity.
Hear me now as I fall on bended knee
My hopes and dreams rest in thee!

JESUS LIVES DEEP WITHIN OUR HEART

Jesus can pardon all of our sin
He can cleanse our souls deep within.
We will no longer be accountable for the past
He'll give us peace to forever last.

Jesus is eternal and all powerful in His ways
His love adds grace and mercy to our days.
He created us and desires us to follow Him
So He can lead us to His Eternal Heavenly realm.

Jesus, our Savior, knows all our heartache and pain
He rescues us from perils time and time again.
We never have to worry as to where He will be
Since He lives deep within the heart of you and me!

JESUS' LOVE

Jesus, our Saviors love is never far
He watches over you no matter where you are.
He will lift you high above to excel
And save your soul from Satan and Hell.

Jesus works both day and night
He never lets you out of His sight
He'll wrap you in His arms tight
Your pathway to Heaven He will light.

Your heart and soul Jesus' love will heal
His grace and wonder working power is real.
He will take your life that is turned upside down
And plant your feet on Holy Ground!

JESUS MAKES ALL THINGS NEW

Put on the full armor of Jesus
Take a stand against Satan's schemes,
Who is always lurking near
To surprise you by all means.

Jesus can overthrow Satan's evil ways
And put him in his place.
He stands ready to bless your days
And overpower Satan thru His grace.

Satan will deceive you
And take you unawares.
Trust Jesus to see you through
He is the one who really cares.

Jesus will stick close beside you until the end
He yearns to be your companion and friend.
Behold He makes all things new
And will have His angels watch over you!

JESUS OFFERS ETERNITY

It thrills my heart to know
That God sent His Son, Jesus, to us long ago
His amazing love to show.

Born of a virgin as a tiny baby at birth
He brought peace and good will to earth
Angels in heaven sang in exaltation, joy and mirth.

Within His tiny body lay salvations plan
That could free every woman and man
All mankind would have a chance to be reborn again.

Jesus taught God's word while living here below
And set many hearts and minds aglow
His awesome love for others kept Him on the go.

He was pure and righteous as could be
Yet judged and condemned to die was He
With no fault found only love in the first degree.

Mocked, betrayed and beaten He bore His cross to Calvary
Nailed there to the cross He shed His precious blood for you and me
So that our souls may forever ransomed be.

Jesus arose from the dead in total victory
And ascended to heaven where love reigns free
All who believe in Him will meet Him there to live eternally!

JESUS, OUR LORD, TAKES AWAY SIN

Oh' Jesus, Lord of all, I praise you
I'm just a sinner begging for life anew
Take my heart and cleanse it thru and thru.

Oh' Jesus, my Savior, who redeemed me
I was sinking deep in sin and you set me free
Now my soul shall forever ransomed be.

Oh' Jesus, you broke the chains that bound me
I know your love and grace will forever be
Thru your awesome power you set me free.

Oh' Jesus, I know you're always near
I feel your presence everywhere
I am so thankful for your never-ending care.

Oh' Jesus, who daily takes away my sin
You have made me happier than I've ever been
By entering my heart and letting your love shine in!

JESUS PAID FOR OUR SINS

Never forget the cross where Jesus shed His blood
He washed away our sins with the healing flood.
We must never forget the love He did freely give
Great was the price He paid so that we may forever live.

It is through Jesus' grace that we are saved
He gave salvation's plan and our pathway to Heaven paved.
Good works alone will never save our soul
We're justified by faith in Jesus and His blood makes us whole.

Works are the fruit of our salvation
Working for Christ fills the heart with joyful elation.
Reach out to others who come into contact with you
Strive to glorify God in all you say or do!

JESUS' PROMICE

Jesus says stay in my will divine
I will share with you all that is mine.
Trust me and stay by my side
Many rich blessings I will provide.

I am the one who created you
My grace will see you through.
Give me complete control
I will change your life and make you whole.

Offer your prayers up to me
I will give you sweet eternity.
Best of all I will give you peace of mind
And contentment in life you will find.

Walk close beside me day and night
I will make your pathway bright.
I wait patiently to hear from you
And stand ready your life to renew!

JESUS PURCHASED MY REDEMPTION

Dear Jesus, thank you for loving me
You purchased my redemption at Calvary.
Your life, your all you willingly gave
You shed your precious blood my soul to save.

I now have been justified and set free
Salvation you give with promise of eternity.
This world is not my final resting place
My eternal home is heaven due to your grace.

I have no condemnation due to my sin
You set me free by cleansing my soul deep within,
And blessed me more than words can tell
Your awesome love serves me so well.

Dear Jesus, you have made me holy without blame
Blessed be God, your Father; I praise His holy name.
Through your grace you took away my sin and shame
Within my life you lit a never ending burning flame!

JESUS, SON OF GOD

Herald angels sing
Of a new born King.
He is Jesus Christ the Lord
And is to be forever adored.

From heaven He came
Jesus is His name.
He's God's only Son
He offers hope to everyone.

Living He administered to His fellowman
He spread His love across this land.
Dying He offered us Salvation's plan
We only have to believe and follow His command.

He died nailed to a cross at Calvary
And His bloods crimson flow,
Cleansed our iniquity to set us free
Washing our hearts as white as snow.

He changed the world thru His act of love
Now our soul shall forever ransomed be.
We shall reign with Him in Heaven above
Forever and ever throughout eternity!

JESUS STANDS BY US

Jesus is our strength and song
Thru His amazing love we are made strong
Within the realm of His grace we belong.

Jesus longs for us to worship Him
He will brighten our days that are dim
And guide us to His heavenly realm.

Jesus will never let us down
Our heart and soul with joy He will crown
His love will keep us safe and sound.

Jesus watches over us night and day
And stands ready to light our way
So we will never go astray!

JESUS TOOK ME IN

I was chained and shackled by sin
Until Jesus my Savior took me in.
His blood cleansed my soul as white as snow
Now His amazing grace I'll forever know.

I am thankful He loved me so much
He set me free from Satan's clutch.
Over death He won total victory
And now offers me sweet eternity.

Jesus shelters me in His love
He promises me a home with Him above.
I praise Him and glorify His name
Precious Lamb of God, He bore all my shame.

Although a high price Jesus had to pay
He took all my transgressions away.
He holds me close beneath His wings
And takes away my sinfulness as my heart joyfully sings!

JESUS TOUCHED ME

Jesus reached out His nail scarred hand to me
Saying come child of mine; I'll set your soul free.
I gently took His precious hand in mine
As I asked Him to save me thru His power divine.

Now that I've found peace and love at last
I'll keep my hand in His nail scarred grasp;
I will never be alone or have to second guess
He will lead me in paths of righteousness.

Jesus touched my soul thru His majesty
And opened my eyes so that I may see
What He had planned for me to be
Over sin and shame, He gave me victory.

I'll cling to Jesus like a branch does to a vine
Until my heart and soul with His doth intertwine.
Then some sweet day I'll reign with Him eternally
In heavens fair land where milk and honey flow free!

JESUS TRANSFORMED MY SOUL

I was shackled by sin and shame
Yet Jesus loved me just the same
Nailed to a cross at Calvary He took my blame.

Jesus came into the heart of me
And transformed my soul for eternity
His grace and love has set my soul free.

When Jesus entered my sin sick heart
He changed my life and gave me a brand new start
From His loving ways I'll never depart.

Jesus loved me before I knew Him
He, my Savior, changed my life that was grim
His amazing love brightened my view that was dim.

Jesus lives in my heart to forever stay
His glorious love shines on me each day
He, Lord of all, will never lead me astray!

JESUS WATCHES OVER ME

My Lord and Savior watches over me
As each day passes His signs I see.
All I have to do is call His name
And He says "my child I am so glad you came".

He is my Savior, the greatest friend I've ever known
And is quick to let me know I am not alone.
All I have to do is turn to him in heartfelt prayer
My many troubles He is willing to share.

Then He takes my heartaches one by one
Until my spirit soars to see I now have none.
I just know He cares and loves me very much
Although I feel so unworthy of His touch!

JESUS WILL CARRY YOU ON

If not for Calvary
Lost forever we would be
Jesus on the bloodstained cross set us free.

The cross is empty and Jesus lives on high
Now and forever His love lingers nigh
We look forward to seeing Him by and by.

Jesus is with us day and night
And will be until our soul takes flight
Then in heaven we'll walk within His light.

He's our Savior who'll never leave us alone
He is the greatest friend we've ever known
And will keep us within His safety zone.

Jesus watches over all we do
His grace is sufficient to see us thru
And His love is forever true.

So when you're lost and alone
And all hope seems to be gone
Trust in Jesus; His love will carry you on!

JESUS WILL MEND OUR BROKEN WAYS

Jesus shed His precious blood
He sacrificed it for our sin.
Praise Him for the crimson flood
That cleansed our souls deep within.

His sacrifice completed the plan of salvation
It is based on faith in Him alone.
He receives all who come to Him in dedication
His love is the greatest comfort ever known.

Christ is ever ready to help us when in need
We should continually offer Him highest praise.
He stands ready our hungry souls to feed
Thru His Grace He mends our broken ways.

Jesus' glory covers the earth as water covers the sea
He freely gives us wisdom and grace each day.
He constantly reaches down to you and me
And longs to guide us the heavenly way!

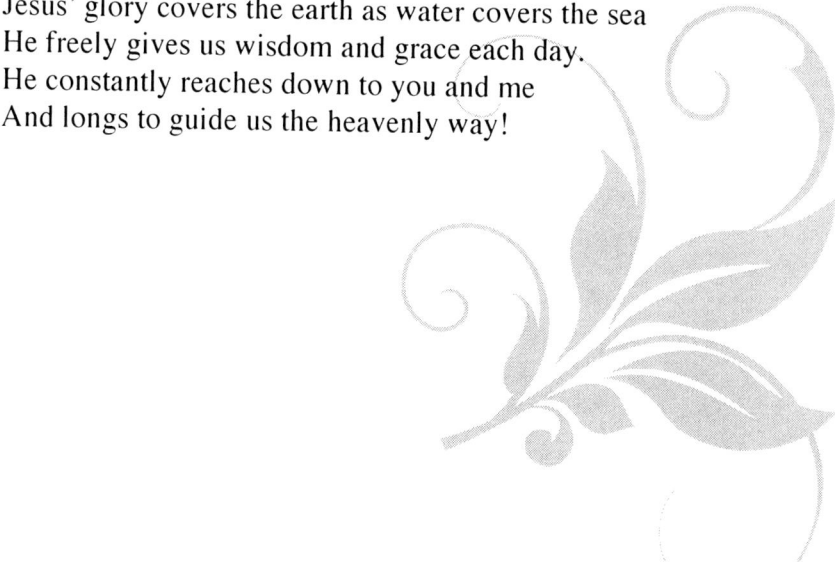

JESUS WILL SEE YOU THROUGH

When you walk with Jesus
Your entire life will change.
He will brighten your pathway
And all your priorities rearrange.

When your days are dark and dreary
And troubles have made you weary,
Jesus' love will make you strong
And fill your heart with joyful song.

When you're downhearted and blue
Jesus will quickly come to your rescue.
He lends His mercy and grace to you
His amazing love will help you make it through.

When all hope you have lost
And your soul is tempest tossed,
If on Jesus' blessed promises you will lean
He stays ever ready to intervene!

JESUS WILL NEVER LET YOU DOWN

Jesus, our Redeemer, will never let you down
Trust Him and he'll surround you with His love renown.
Believe in Him and take Him at His word
Your soul with His Armor He will gird.

Feast on His goodness and mercy that He lends
Baste in His amazing love and grace that never ends.
Offer prayers and thanks unto to Him
He will light your path to never grow dim.

Reach out to others and guide them God's way
Be a beacon for Him that brightly shines each day.
Move forward as a Christian and don't look back
Depend on His divine guidance to keep you on track!

JESUS WILL RESCUE YOU

When troubles come along
It's hard to be strong.
Jesus can rescue you from the fieriest storm
And wrap you in His arms safe and warm.

He will never leave or forsake you
His love will see you through.
His grace He freely lends
With peace and mercy that never ends.

Jesus can plant your feet on higher ground
He is easy to be found since He stays around.
He lingers close beside you ever so near
Just call on Him and He will hear.

Jesus will bless your life
And take away your sin and strife.
He'll keep you safely in His embrace
And save your soul through His grace!

JESUS WILL REVIVE US AGAIN

Jesus witnesses our short comings
Yet He always forgives them.
He looks at us and smiles
And offers His grace and love to overwhelm.

Jesus embraces us in His arms each day
He, thru His amazing love, never turns us away.
When we turn to Him, He gives sweet relief
He takes residence in our heart to heal our grief.

Jesus will reach out and hold our hand
He'll lift us up to help us stand.
When our heart is burdened with a heavy load
He will walk each step with us down the rocky road.

Jesus gives us freedom from fear and shame
He's the master healer who takes our blame.
We must let go of our heartache and pain
Give it to Jesus; He stands ready to revive us again!

JESUS WILL SEE YOU THROUGH

Many times around ourselves we build a wall
Then when dark shadows around us fall,
We don't have the strength to stand tall
And have no friends on whom to call.

However, there's one who loves us more than life
It's Jesus who died to redeem us by taking our sin and strife.
He's always available and hears our every prayer.
We only have to call on Him and He will hear.

Jesus' love is forever pure and true
And He watches over all that we, His children, do.
If only we will believe and trust in Him
He will brighten our days that have grown dim!

KNEEL IN PRAYER

Kneel in admiration for prayer
Jesus will meet you there
He waits to wrap you in his care.

Praise Him for giving Salvation
Glorify Him in heartfelt dedication
He will fill your soul with inspiration.

Kneel before Jesus this very day
Ask Him to take your sins away
Invite Him into your heart to stay.

Honor Him as Savior and King
Lift up your voice to Him and sing
Accept the joy His love doth bring!

LAMB OF GOD, MY PRINCE OF PEACE

Lamb of God, I dearly love you
I shall worship you my entire life thru.
You are my most sacred dwelling place
Who stands beside me no matter what I face.

You're my Precious Redeemer and Prince of Peace
Your amazing love gives me sweet release.
On your promises I will forever stand
Just guide me and hold tightly to my hand.

Lord of all, I crown you as my King
With joy you make my heart sing
Keep me tucked safely beneath thy wing
I cherish your love above everything.

Lord of my life, my Master and Guide
In the shadow of your love I'll always hide
I'll be happy so long as you stay by my side
Your presence fills my heart with deep pride!

LET JESUS COME INTO YOUR HEART

Walk with Jesus each day
He will guide you in the perfect way.
Take your burdens to Him in prayer
He will keep them in His care.

Jesus yearns to live within your heart
His loving ways He wants to impart.
Open your heart and let Him come in
He will take away all your sin.

When you're troubled with no one to turn to
Jesus stands available to help you.
He'll wrap you in His arms of love
And lift your spirit higher than you've dreamed of!

LET LOVE REIGN

Love is the bond of perfection
Honor it above all as a beautiful reflection.
Keep the peace of God within your heart
Let it rule deep down within your inner most part.

Love binds us together to make us whole
It's the golden chain that heals the soul.
Love keeps us in God's care
It builds a haven to escape hell's despair.

Let love reign in your heart right away
God's peace will come into your life to stay.
Give God all glory and follow His will
He will make your heart quiet and still!

LIFE IS FLEETING

Life is fleeting and we will soon pass away
But if we persevere and live for Jesus each day
Unto heaven He shall pave our way.

Just lift your heart to Him and say a prayer
He's always available and lingers near
He loves all of His children; to Him we are dear.

Do not tarry and never wait
Soon it may be too late
Your heart and soul to Him you must dedicate.

Jesus' love will guide you through life's way
And change your darkest night to day
Ask Him right now to come into your heart to stay!

LIFT ME UP LORD

Lord of all, take my hand
Lift me up; help me stand
As I travel thru this weary land.

Oh' God, the great and mighty one
Hold me tight until victory over sin is won
Walk close beside me until life on earth is done.

Sweet Jesus, lend me thy grace and mercy
Cleanse my soul of iniquity and set me free
Intertwine with me until I become one with thee.

Precious Savior, have compassion on me, a sinner
My heart and soul I open for you to enter
Guide me safely to thy majestic kingdoms center!

LITTLE HUMMINGBIRD

Little hummingbird you're such an alluring sight
With iridescent colors gleaming in the sunlight.
You're so tiny hovering through the air
As you search for sweet nectar everywhere.

No bigger than a butterfly
You come swiftly darting by.
I watch as you pierce each beautiful flower
And gather sweet nectar to sustain your power.

Little hummingbird, I never hear you sing
As other birds that fly on wing,
Yet you have an amazing humming sound
Each time you are air bound and flying around.

Every time I get you in my sight
You quickly take off in flight,
But blissful moments you leave behind
That stay recessed deep within my heart and mind!

LOCK JESUS WITHIN YOUR HEART

Reach out and touch the nail scarred hand
There's healing in it you'll never understand
Jesus will caress you with His love so grand.

Walk within the light of His majestic love
Experience joy that you never dreamed of
He rains down blessings from heaven above.

Reach out and touch Jesus' hand today
He is the truth, the light and the way
Lock Him deep within your heart to forever stay!

LONGING FOR HEAVEN

Lord, hold thy own heart next to mine
Fill it with your pure sweet love genuine.
I'm just a mere mortal on this earth
I long for my heavenly home and rebirth.

Lord, I can barely wait to see your face
Just lend me your mercy and grace,
Until my spirit travels thru starry skies
To be with you in heavenly paradise.

Lord, I lift your name on high
For saving my soul that shall never die.
You're the greatest thing that ever happened to me
Your gift of salvation offers promise of sweet eternity!

LORD, DIRECT MY PATH

Father, God, thank you for your Son
Thru His love my salvation has been won
He is Lord of all; the anointed one.

Thank you Jesus for giving me victory
Your grace and love has set me free
My sins have been forgiven due to thy mercy.

Lord, direct my path; keep me free from sin
Open my heart and let your love shine in
Cleanse my soul deep within.

Lord, keep me headed in your direction
Purify my soul to holy perfection
It is my desire to show others Godly affection!

LORD, DRAW ME NEAR

Lord, draw me nearer; keep me in line
Hold this heart of mine closer to thine
Bind me next to you with thy holy twine.

When trials come and dark shadows blind me
The beauty of your divine light is all I can see
I know your amazing love will set me free.

Dearest Jesus, I claim you as my very own
I'm so glad I have you to lean on
You're the greatest friend I've ever known.

Within my life you are a vital part
I keep you tucked deep within my heart
So thy loving ways you can impart.

Lord, just draw me nearer than ever before
Rain down thy bountiful blessings galore
Lead me homeward to heaven's door!

LORD, HELP ME MAKE IT THROUGH

Lord, please hold my hand
Lift me up and help me stand.
My life is dark and dreary
And I am so tired and weary.

Lord, I can't make it without you
Your love is needed to see me through.
Insert thy power and be my guiding light
Blot out all darkness and restore my sight.

Lord, please hold my hand
Guide me safely across this troubled land.
The mountains are high and the valleys deep
Without your love life's outlook is bleak.

Lord, please hold tight to my hand
Help me to forever stand.
Guide me safely to heavens shore
To reign with thee forevermore!

LORD, I NEED YOU

Lord, strengthen me to walk in thy spirit
Protect me from evil and corrupt ways.
I commit myself wholly to you
Hold me with your strong hand always.

Thank you Father for the gift of your Son
Who gave His life to redeem everyone.
You made my darkest day bright
When you sent Jesus as my guiding light.

Lord, help me to be all you desire me to be
Forgive me of my sins and cast out all iniquity.
Give me peace and joy within my soul
You and you alone can make me whole.

Open my eyes and allow me to see
Glimpses of your love and majesty.
I desperately need you to be my guide
I'll be satisfied as long as you're by my side!

LORD, REVEAL THINE OWN WAY

Lord of all, show me the way
Help me to walk closer to you each day.
I want to be forever yielded to you
Take my heart and soul as yours to renew.

I want to bask within thy grace and love
Rain them down on me from above.
It is my aim to always glorify you
I will praise you for your love so true.

Lord of all; reveal Thine own way to me
Show me exactly what you want me to be.
I want to magnify your name above all
And shall be ever listening for your call!

LOVE SO AWESOME AND TRUE

Lord, my heart seeks after you
Give me a Christ like spirit in all that I do.
Drive the truth of your word deep within my heart
Bend my stubborn will as your loving ways you impart.

Lord, keep me from selfishness and conceit
Help me to esteem all others that I meet.
Make my trembling heart quiet and still
As I seek after thy glory and divine will.

Lord, give me wisdom I've always dreamed of
Fill my heart with thy compassion and love.
Mold me and make me into what you want me to be
Help me project thy Holy Spirit for all to see.

Lord, your love is awesome and true
No one else can touch my life like you.
Make me strong enough to win Satan's fight
Keep me walking in thy blessed love light!

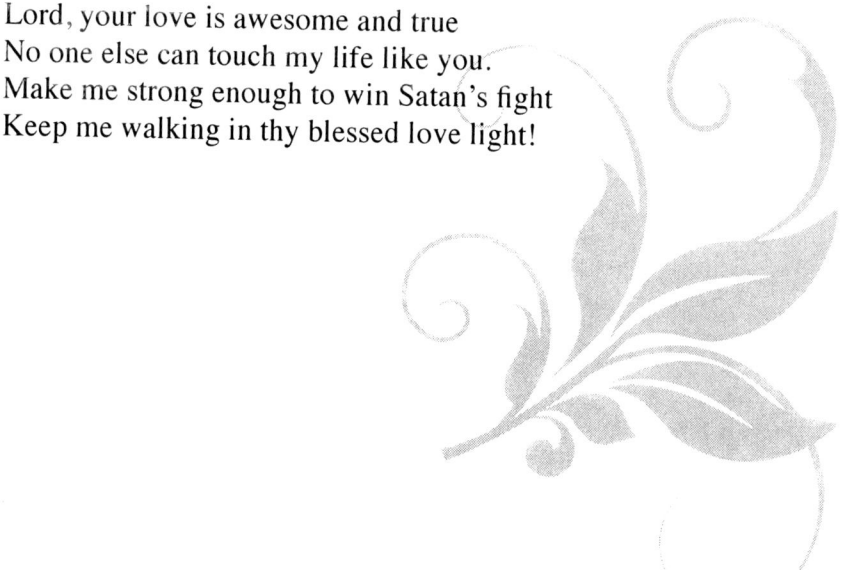

LOVE THAT SERVES YOU WELL

Reach out and grasp the nail scarred hand
Walk with Jesus across this land
With His holiness your life He will brand.

Surround yourself with His love and grace
He will lock you within His warm embrace
And guide you towards His heavenly place.

Glorify and praise Him in joyful song
Trust Him each night thru and all day long
His wonder working power will keep you strong.

Jesus loves you more than words can tell
His amazing grace and love will serve you well
As your Savior He will rescue you from Satan's hell!

MAGNIFY THE LORD

God deserves our continual praise
He blesses us in so many ways.
I invite you to worship and praise Him
His love your heart and soul will overwhelm.

Magnify the Lord all the time
He'll bind you next to Him with holy twine.
He can perfect you as no one else can
Through love He freely gives Salvation's plan.

God diligently seeks your soul
So Satan won't have control.
He's your Savior and will never forsake you
His love and devotion is forever true!

MAJESTIC BEAUTY OF SNOW

This morning I awoke to a wonderful surprise
Beautiful snow floated softly from the skies.
The tree tops and lands were all aglow
With majestic beauty of fallen snow.

Like crystal tear drops snow kept floating down
Until it covered the earth in wondrous beauty renown.
Blanketed in a coat of white that is rarely seen
The hills and valleys look so pristine and clean.

We serve an awesome God in so many ways
He never fails to love us and bless our days.
Rich blessings He sends our hearts and minds to amaze
I glorify God for His bountiful love and give Him highest praise!

MARVELOUS GRACE

Grace, grace, marvelous grace
You can witness it every place
As through this hectic life you race.

Grace that God lends to us all
Grace to lift us when we fall
He lends it as on Him we call.

Grace is more majestic than anything we receive
If we follow Jesus and on Him believe
His love enters our heart never more to leave.

Grace lifts our spirits to heights unknown
It's a free gift given by our Savior alone
Grace will cleanse our soul and carry us home!

MISSING MOM

Mom, your voice echoes in the wind
It seems I'll meet you right around the bend.
One thing is certain you loved me well
You taught me all about life and how to excel.

Mom, it's for sure I miss you more each day
I look for your shadow all along life's way.
My longing to be near you will never end
You were my mother, teacher and best friend.

Mom, I can still feel your hand holding mine
As you did so many years ago back in time.
Come what may, you looked out for me
And filled my heart with sweet love and serenity.

Mom, I search and search for your face in vain
Yearning to hold you close once again.
As time goes by I miss you more and more
And wish we could hug as we did so many times before.

Mom, God had a special plan for you
He needed you to brighten heavens view.
He could have searched the world over
And never found another like you!

MORE LIKE THEE LORD

Lord Jesus, I want to be
Free from sin and more like thee.
Take this fainting heart of mine
Bind it next to thine.

Fill it with thy pure sweet love
Lift me to loftier heights above.
Fill my empty cup to the brim
Light my path that has grown dim.

Shelter me in your love and grace
As thru this hectic life I race.
Walk with me thru the darkest night
Be my beacon as you shed your light.

Lord Jesus, lead me every day
Then never more will I stray.
Oh' what a thrill it will be
To be made more like thee!

MY BEACON IN THE NIGHT

I traveled a dark and dreary road
Burdened down with a heavy load
Due to frustrations life had bestowed.

I met my Savior along the way
He banished all my darkness away
Then He came into my heart to stay.

He took my troubles one by one
Until suddenly I realized I had none
Thru His divine intervention victory was won.

My Savior is my beacon in the night
He protects me thru His power and might
And I'll walk forever within His love light!

MY BLESSINGS FROM GOD

As I go to my garden each day
I can tell Dear God; you've stepped my way.
Your love is reflected in all that I see
I sense a touch of your divine majesty.

When I look upon the flowers wet with dew
I realize there is no one greater than you.
You bless me with so many wonderful things
My heart with rapture sings.

As I listen to the song birds in the trees
I am touched by their sweet melodies.
Within my life you give hope and peace
And offer undying love that shall never cease.

Your love follows me no matter where I go
Through countless blessings that set my life aglow.
I feel the touch of your warm embrace
And you fill my heart with thy sweet grace.

I'll shout your love from now on
And tell how your precious blood for sin does atone.
When my earthly life is over and done
Take me to your haven of rest O' Holy One!

MY FATHER, GOD

My Father, God, you're worthy of my praise
I am so grateful to be a child of you, the King.
Help me to walk in your spirit and emulate your ways
Great is the hope and peace into life you bring.

Lord of all, I will always worship you
You're my comforter whose love is true.
Unto you I shall forever cling
You make my heart joyfully sing.

My Father, God, I'll glorify you thru joyful songs
For unto you my heart and soul belongs.
I'll forever praise you for giving me Salvation
And shout your name in acclamation!

MY GREATEST SENSATION

Dear Jesus, help me turn away from possessiveness
Let me give more to others and you.
You're always near; I never have to second guess
When I need you, you quickly come to the rescue.

Dearest Jesus, I put my life in your hands and trust you
May your peace and truth guard this heart of mine?
Your spiritual blessings always see me through
You paid a debt you didn't owe to redeem me by thy power divine.

Dear Jesus, I rest in peace because you saved me
You changed me through the power of your cross.
Now my soul shall forever ransomed be
My massive debt of sin you paid so I wouldn't be lost.

Dear Jesus, thank you for your compassion for a lost world
All sin and shame for lost sinners on you were hurled.
You offer hope through your gift of salvation
I praise you in your majesty as my greatest sensation!

MY GUIDING LIGHT

Lord, I'm so happy in my life you live
Thank you for the strength you give.
Take this heart of mine
It's yours to control and refine.

Lord, cleanse my soul through thy power divine
Fill it to the brim with your love genuine.
Take me within thy loving embrace
Shed on me your wonder working grace.

Lord, I praise you for thy mercy and love
And the rich blessings you rain down from above.
There's no way I can ever thank you enough
For rescuing me when the going gets rough.

Lord, I glorify you in your awesome ways
You're always faithful to send your healing rays.
When life gets chaotic and I can't cope
You're my guiding light who gives me hope!

MY HEART WITH RAPTURE SOARS

Thank you Jesus for loving me
You died for my sins to set me free.
I am so blessed to know
That I am your child and you love me so.

Your mercy and sweet love
You constantly send from above.
Amazing is the grace that you send
And undying is your love with no end.

Dear Jesus, I seek to follow your will
Purify my heart; make me quiet and still.
Release me from all guilt and shame
Light within my life a Godly flame.

My Jesus, make me pure and clean for you
Wash me and cleanse me thru and thru.
I am so happy to be a child of yours
Until my heart with rapture soars!

MY HEART'S SONG

Today I gazed at the skies of blue
With puffy white clouds touched in silver hue
And dear God, I thought of you.

Then I saw flowers in beauty rare
And smelled their fragrance in the air
While beautiful butterflies fluttered near.

Birds were chirping and singing merrily
While flying back and forth from tree to tree
It was such a beautiful sight to see.

Nature's majestic beauty thrills me so
Until it leaves me with a pleasant afterglow
Which lifts my spirits when tired and slow.

God is the great and mighty creator of all I see
He, my Savior, is my heart's song and shall forever be
I will worship and praise Him forever in His deity!

MY HOPE AND SALVATION

Lord you mean so much to me
Draw me ever close to thee.
Take me on the road that you're on
So I will never have to walk alone

Lord, all I possess is a gift from you
My heart and soul is yours to renew.
Thank you for your power in my life
You took away my sin and strife.

Lord, I bless your holy name
Within my life you have lit a flame.
You are my hope and salvation
Unto you I offer my utmost dedication!

MY LORD AND KING

Lord, I am so glad
You're a part of me.
I will worship you forever
In your divine majesty.

Hold me close; keep me near
Cast away my heartache and fear.
Every song that I sing
I dedicate to you my Lord and King.

Lord, control every move I make
Watch over each step that I take.
Your divine guidance is needed so
Be with me every place I go.

Every treasure that I hold
All my silver and my gold,
I offer to you and all that I am
It's yours my Precious Lamb.

As I think of Calvary
And the price you paid for me
Just to set my sinful soul free
I praise you in your deity!

MY MASTER, REDEEMER AND FRIEND

Oh' Jesus, Lord of all, I praise you
I'm just a sinner begging for mercy
Take my heart, cleanse it thru and thru.

Oh' Jesus, my Savior, I know you'll love me forever
I was lost; you found me and brought me safely in
And bound me with chords no one can sever.

Oh' Jesus, I know you're near
I feel your presence everywhere
I am so thankful for your love and care.

Oh' Jesus, keep me close to your heart
So when hard times come and teardrops start
Your loving ways you can impart.

Oh' Jesus, who takes away all sin
I'm so happy you live in my heart deep within
And that you're my Master, Redeemer and friend!

MY OWN EARTHLY ANGEL

DEDICATED TO MY DAUGHTER, ALICE LUCAS GOODING

Many years ago it came as no surprise
When God sent me a little angel in disguise.
A baby daughter named Alice for me to hold near
She brought joy to my life every single year.

Now she is a fine lady whose love is so rare
And she watches over me with tender care.
God knew what He was doing when He sent her to me
Now and forever my little angel she shall be.

She checks on me day and night
Enhancing my life as she assures things go right.
Thank you God for your intervention from above
In sending me Alice, my little angel, and her sweet love!

MY SALVATION

The Lord is my salvation
He's my strength and my song.
I will praise Him thru the night
And all the day long.

I will lift up my voice
Across this land,
And shout in acclamation
Of His love so grand.

My salvation He gives free
And His love is no mystery.
I cherish my fellowship with Him
He guides me toward His Heavenly realm!

MY SAVIOR WILL NEVER FORSAKE ME

I have a Savior who lives in my heart today
He's there forever no matter what man may say
He is my Blessed Redeemer who is there to stay.

When life is tempest tossed and my heart is breaking
He is faithful to relieve the pain and aching
Just to let me know that I have not been forsaken.

There's no way I could make it in life without Him
He light's my path when storms rage and life is grim
Through His Love He fills my empty cup to the brim.

My Savior will never let me go astray
Since He stays close beside me night and day
His grace and mercy will always lead me His way!

MY SAVIOR'S LOVE

I serve a living Savior
He hears me when I pray.
And intervenes in my life
To take my heartaches away.

When I'm in deep despair
And life is tempest tossed,
He shelters me within His love
To assure me all is not lost.

Just the time I need Him
He stands willing and ready,
To show His love and calm me down
As He eases my pain and makes life steady.

There's no way I could make it
If not for my Savior and the love of Him.
My life would be so empty
My path would be dark and dim.

My Savior stays ever near
And available for me to call on.
He wraps me in His warm embrace
Until all my fear and grief is gone!

MY SECRET HIDING PLACE

Within God's realm I have a secret hiding place
There He lends His mercy and amazing grace
To carry me through this world's hectic race.

In my secret hiding place I feel safe and secure
God gently lifts my burdens my aching heart to cure
As He shares His majestic love so sweet and pure.

When troubles come and darkness covers my face
I slip quietly away to my secret hiding place
Just to get a brand new supply of God's mercy and grace.

God is the joy of my life when in sorrows I almost drown
He never fails to meet me no matter where and never lets me down
He quickly surrounds me with the beauty of His love renown!

NO, I'M NOT DEAD

No, I haven't died
Heaven's pearly gates are open wide
I have entered and am safely inside
I'm there evermore to abide.

I'm singing and shouting in jubilation
Thanking Jesus for my salvation.
I'm so grateful for the price He paid for me
It thrills my soul as His blessed face I see.

There's no reason for you to mourn or cry
I'm in heaven never more to die.
My spirit has soared to that celestial land above
I shall be sheltered eternally beneath God's wings of love!

ONLY GOD IS WORTHY OF PRAISE

God, my Father, I honor your name
Within my life you have lit a burning flame.
Only you are worthy of worship, glory and praise
It is my desire to honor you all of my days.

Lord of all, make my life count for thee
Until I reach thy heavenly place prepared for me.
With all my heart and soul, I want to glorify you
Help me bless others in all I say and do.

Precious Redeemer, I'm so glad you set me free
You have given a spiritual inheritance to me,
Making it possible for me to reign with you above
I am a blessed person because of your love.

King of all Kings, my life you haft blest
Guide me to thy eternal home of perfect rest.
Just keep your blessings continually flowing
As I witness to others while thru life I am going.

Wonderful Savior, keep me acceptable in thy sight
Keep me walking within thy perfect light.
Tame my tongue and change my heart
Open my eyes to thy glories; give me a brand new start!

ON THE WINGS OF A DOVE

God sent me a message of love
On the wings of a pure white dove,
So beautiful in his splendor
He lit right outside my window.

The beautiful white dove came to give me hope
I needed divine intervention in order to cope.
I'm so thankful God cares so much
That He sends awesome signs our lives to touch.

My soul was burdened in despair
With more trials than I could bear.
Many things in life I fail to understand
But I know God, in His grace, lends a healing hand!

OPEN MY EYES LORD

Open my eyes Lord that I may see
Thy awesome mercies you rain on me.
Take my heart and cleanse it thru and thru
Make me more like you.

I praise you for your intervention from above
And thank you for your unconditional love.
Father, God, I fully understand
Riches come from only your hand.

Lord, you are the King of Glory; the great I Am
You're my Savior; the Sacrificial Lamb.
Heavenly Father, I am so glad you loved me
So much you died at Calvary to set my soul free.

My lips shall praise you in your majesty
For thy amazing love that shall forever be.
Hold me close, keep me next to thee
I can hardly wait your blessed face to see!

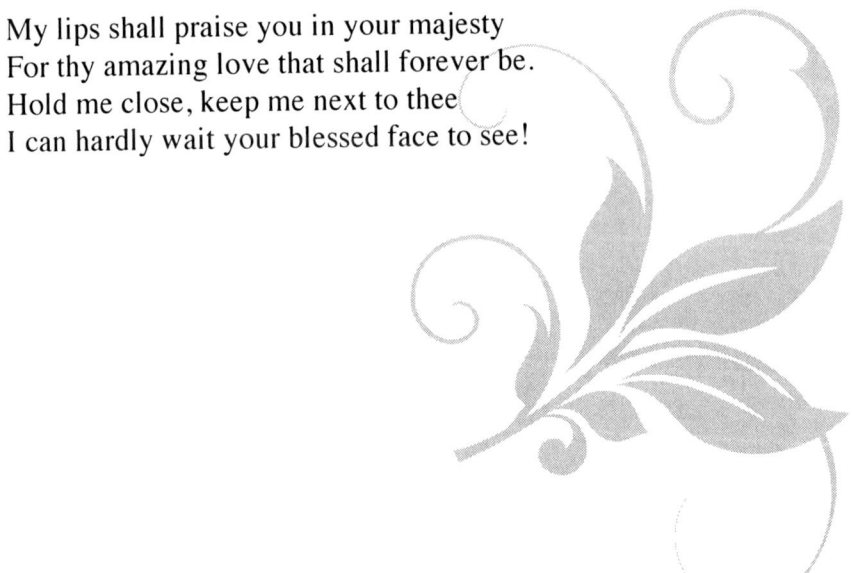

OPEN MY EYES LORD AND LET ME SEE

Lord, may I use my talents to glorify you
In all that I endeavor to do,
Since they are not really mine
You have blest me with them thru thy love divine.

Fill my heart with thy sweet love
Rain it down to me from above,
So I may share it with others free
As I walk within the divine light of thee.

Lord, my heart and soul unto you I yield
Set before me the goals you want fulfilled.
Help me to follow thy good and perfect way
Forgive me of my transgressions each day.

Inspire me to portray thy love and goodness
Grant that I share it some other soul to bless
Open my eyes and let me see
Glimpses of truth you have for me!

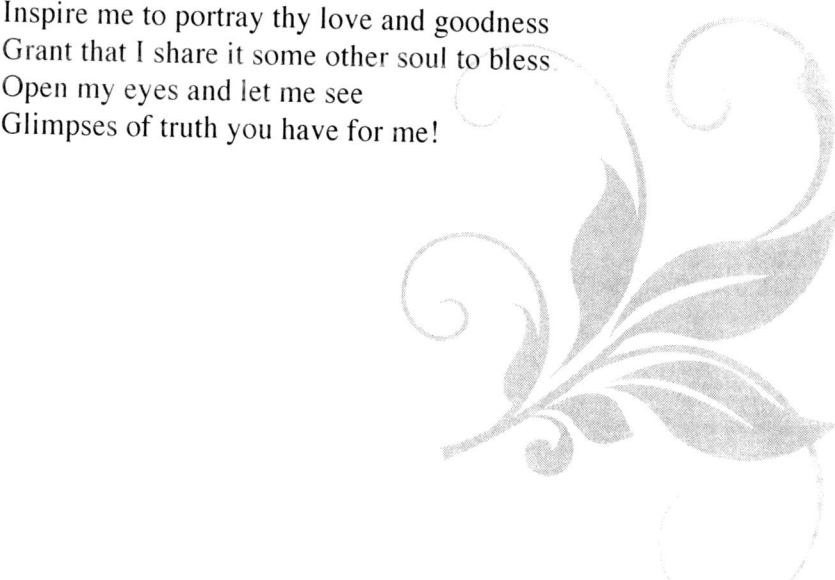

OUR HEAVENLY HOME

When our final course on earth is run
There's a place beyond the setting sun
Where victory over death is won.

Our heavenly home awaits us there
Jesus, our Savior, will take us in His care
In that beautiful celestial land so fair.

It's a land that is majestic and bright
There's no darkness for Jesus is the light
And scores of angels are in flight.

Ransomed forever our soul shall be
We shall reign with God, our Father, throughout eternity
In that sweet land where milk and honey flow free!

OUR ONLY SALVATION

Jesus always lingers nigh
Although His home is in heaven on high.
He pleads with you and me
More like Him to be.

Jesus is our only source of salvation
He desires our soul in dedication.
Trust and believe in His powers
Great blessings on us He showers.

Please do not tarry or wait
Believe Him now! Tomorrow may be too late.
Accept Him deep within your heart and soul
His amazing love will make you whole.

Trust Jesus and take Him at His word
Your heart and soul with His Armor He will gird.
He'll thrill you with His gift of eternity
In heaven where milk and honey flow free!

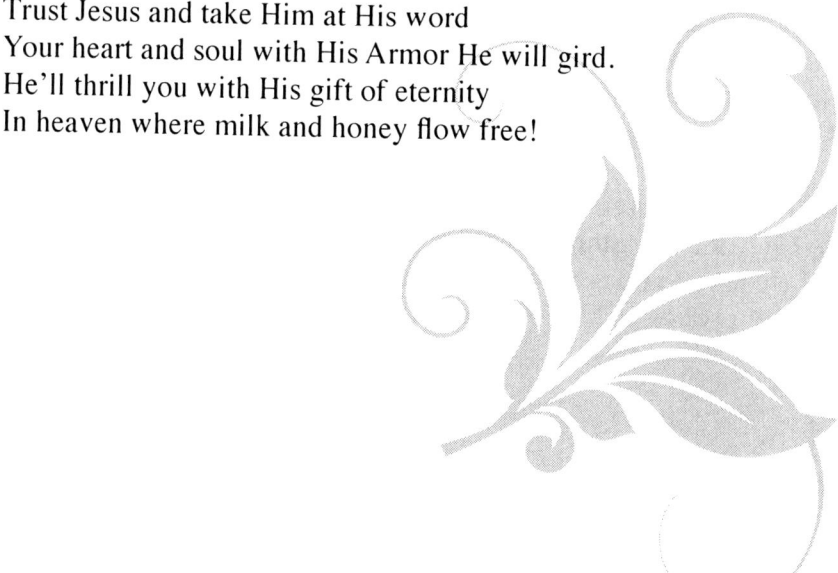

OUR SHIELD AND DEFENDER

We are spiritual heirs of Jesus
He died on the cross for our sin.
All we have to do is believe in Him
And open our hearts to let Him in.

Jesus paid a debt
He did not owe,
And willingly gave His life
His awesome love to show.

Jesus changed our life
Through the power of the cross.
He took away our sin and strife
So we would not be lost.

Jesus gives eternal salvation to you and me
Although we are as unworthy as can be.
He loved us ere we knew Him
And lights our path when dim.

Jesus knew we were sinners in need of a Savior
So He made the ultimate sacrifice in our favor.
All we have to do is believe in Him and surrender
He will save us and become our Shield and Defender!

OUR SOURCE OF SALVATION IS JESUS

Jesus is the source of eternal Salvation
For all who trust and obey Him in dedication.
He was designated by God, His Father, above
To rescue us from darkness by showing His love.

Jesus willingly gave His life nailed to a cross at Calvary
His precious atoning blood He freely shed for you and me.
It can wash away all of our vilest sins and set us free
Our souls shall forever ransomed be to live eternally.

Jesus stands ready to let His love light shine within
Our heart and soul to take away all shame and sin.
If we believe and trust in Him as thru life we go
His redeeming love and grace is ours to know!

PRAISE AND GLORIFY GOD

Join in with the heavenly jubilation
Praise God in joyful adoration.
Sing unto Him of His greatness
Bow before Him your sins to confess.

God will never leave you or let you down
With goodness and mercy your soul He will crown.
Glorify the beauty of His majesty and holiness
He gives victory over sin your life to bless.

Sing songs of praise to Him as Christ the King
Lift up your voice and let it joyfully ring.
He will keep you singing throughout eternity
In His heavenly home prepared for you and me!

PRAISE GOD IN HIS DIETY

Our God is awesome in His ways
He works miracles and deserves our praise.
Although we go through many tests in life
He's always near to help us resolve our strife.

God in His wisdom knows how much we can take
He watches us when we're sleeping and awake.
If we listen to Him and make His ways our choice
In the mist of difficult times He causes us to rejoice.

God can create a clean heart in you and me
He'll open our eyes His glories to see.
Just glorify His name and praise Him in His deity
He will make us pure and holy as He sets us free.

Thank you God for being merciful and true
You gave your life our soul to save and our life to renew.
We love you dearly and your name we magnify
We treasure your love and lift your name on high!

PROMISE OF ETERNITY

Although Jesus' death was a tragedy
His amazing love transformed you and me.
By His stripes we are healed
Our fate He forever sealed.

He took our guilt and sin away
And planted our feet on higher ground to stay.
We are so blessed He loved you and me
He gives us an opportunity to live eternally.

Jesus will guide us safely to His heavenly realm
All we have to do is believe and trust in Him.
He will shelter us forever within the balm of His love
And take us to heights we've never dreamed of!

RELY ON JESUS

Rely on Jesus' courage and power
Great are the blessings He doth shower.
He can lift you higher than you've ever been
And give you bountiful joy deep within.

Jesus loves you more than words can tell
His love will always serve you well.
He stands ready for you to call on
He wants to claim you as His own.

Believe on Jesus and trust Him to deliver you
He will guard your life with His love so true.
He died on a cross at Calvary for you and me
To transform us and set our souls free.

Jesus spilt His precious blood long ago
So His saving grace we may know.
His love is more precious than anything.
Rely on Him as your Master, Lord and King!

REVIVED WITH A SPIRITUAL FLAME

Lord, I give unto thy keep
All that is and what's yet to be.
My soul rejoices in thy love so deep
As I walk thru this land and trust thee.

Lord, I know that your love is genuine
I am so proud to be a child of thine.
You fill my heart and soul with serenity
My troubles are no longer what they used to be.

Lord, you took them one by one
Until suddenly I realized I had none.
You took all of my sin and shame
And revived my soul with your spiritual flame!

SALVATION FREE

We praise you Father, God, for all that you have done
Most of all we praise you for the gift of Jesus, your Son
Who ministered on earth and died to redeem everyone.

We praise Jesus for dying on the cross at Calvary
His precious blood He shed to atone for sins of you and me
Now and forever we are offered Salvation free.

We praise Jesus for His crimson bloods healing flow
That washed away sin to make our hearts as white as snow
His amazing grace and power we shall forever know.

We praise the Father, God, and Jesus, His Son, who loved us so
And touched our lives forever with an inner glow
Giving us stamina needed as through this weary life we go.

<u>Stanza</u>

Praise the Father, God, Praise Jesus, His precious Son
Praise them for grace so free and all they have done
Praise and magnify them for Salvation's victory won!

SALVATIONS PLAN

Thank you Jesus for your grace that is greater than all sin
Your amazing love allowed salvations plan to move in.
Thank you Father for giving me thy strength and power
Awesome are the blessings on me that you shower.

Lord of all, forgive me of my sins; make me holy like you
Change this heart of mine and cleanse my soul thru and thru.
Shine the beauty of your love deep within my being
Give me a song to sing and keep me ever singing.

Dear Jesus, it was such a cruel death you had to die
When you shed your blood to save sinners such as I.
I'll forever glorify and praise you for loving me
Over sin and shame, you gave me total victory!

SATISFIED WITH JESUS

Satisfied, satisfied, I'm satisfied with Jesus
He's my Savior who is my one and all.
Satisfied, satisfied, I'm satisfied with Jesus
I'm so glad I listened to His call.

Satisfied, satisfied, I'm satisfied with Jesus
My heart and soul He has won.
Satisfied, satisfied, I'm satisfied with Jesus.
He's God's only Son, the anointed one!

Satisfied, satisfied, I'm satisfied with His healing
His love and mercy to me is so appealing.
He gave my heart and soul a special touch
And let me know He, my Redeemer, loved me so much!

SAVED BY GRACE

I am merely a sinner saved by grace
On the cross at Calvary Jesus took my place.
His life was pure and free from sin
He chose to shed His blood my soul to win.

I am so thankful He loved me
Enough to give me salvation free
From sin and shame, He gave me victory
My soul shall forever ransomed be.

All you have to do is believe and trust Him
Your heart and soul He will overwhelm
He will light your path that is dim
And lead you towards His heavenly realm!

SAVED BY HIS GRACE

I was just a sinner until Jesus redeemed me
He shed His precious blood and cleansed my iniquity
Now my soul shall forever ransomed be.

I am so glad Jesus developed a love relationship with me
He gives me directions for living my life daily
He blesses me through His awesome love and mercy.

Jesus knows I need His helping hand most of all
So He always lingers near and listens for my call
So he can lift me up and help me stand tall!

SEEK HIS FACE

If you're traveling a lonesome road
With your path dark and a heavy load;
Reach out to Jesus and He'll meet you there
He's always looking out for your welfare.

He will lift your burdens as His to bear
And place your heartaches in His care.
You'll walk in the sunshine of His love
And glorify Him as your Father above.

Lift your heart and praise Him without cease
He will give you sweet release.
Without His love you will be forever at a loss
He can change you thru the power of His cross.

Open your heart and let Jesus come in
He will take away all your sin.
He will save you through His wondrous grace
All you have to do is seek His face!

SEEK JESUS

When your life is troubled
And you need sweet release,
Call on Jesus Christ our Savior
He will give you joy and peace.

Just go to Jesus silently in prayer
He will place your heartaches in His care.
He is your Redeemer and the keeper of your soul
His grace and love will make you whole.

Never doubt Jesus' power and love
He will lift you to your loftiest height above.
Believe and trust in Him as you seek His face
He will bless you through His love and grace!

SHE IS NOT DEAD

She's not dead but only gone
She has met Jesus in her heavenly home.
She merely stepped away
To a land that is fairer than day.

Her spirit soared thru the skies
To be with Jesus in paradise
Where the soul never dies
And there will be no more sad goodbyes.

She patiently waits for us there
She is sheltered safely within God's care.
She's happier than she has ever been
In that sweet haven where there is no sin.

So wipe the tears from your eyes
And forget about your earthly ties.
Believe and trust in Jesus to see you thru
He waits patiently to hear from you.

Reach out and take His nail scarred hand
He'll guide you to His celestial land,
Where you'll be reunited with your loved one
When your life on earth is over and done!

SHELTERED IN GOD'S GRACE

Jesus had so much love for His fellowman
He died to give us salvations plan.
He was nailed to a cross at Calvary
And shed His blood to redeem you and me.

Jesus' blood washed our sins away
Oh' what a wonderful and glorious day.
Now our souls shall forever ransomed be
Since His precious blood set us free.

Jesus arose from the grave in victory
He ascended to heaven and offers us eternity.
If we believe in Him and give Him highest praise
He will intervene with God for our sinful ways.

When death takes us, our spirit to Heaven will soar
We shall reign with God, our Savior, forever more.
Heartache and pain will be a thing of the past
We'll be sheltered in God's grace that shall forever last!

SHELTERED IN GOD'S LOVE

I am so glad Jesus loved me
So much He bore the cross at Calvary
From sin and shame to set me free
My soul He ransomed forever thru eternity.

I am so glad God loved me
He sacrificed His Son to set me free
Jesus, His Son, shed His blood willingly
He took away my sins and redeemed me.

I am so glad salvation is free
Jesus, my Savior, promised me eternity,
In His mansion in the sky above
Where I shall be sheltered forever in His love!

SHIRLEY IS NOT GONE

IN MEMORY OF MY SISTER, SHIRLEY B. KNEECE

Shirley is not dead, she's only gone
And has arrived in her eternal home
There she will never walk alone.

Her spirit has winged its flight
To where Jesus is the light
And there is no night.

She has entered heaven's pearly gates
Where Jesus, her Savior, patiently waits
And there'll be no more pain and heartaches.

Jesus walks with her hand in hand
In that beautiful celestial land
And she has met up with the angel band.

Shirley has only left for a short while
Someday soon we'll see that sweet smile
That has always been her special style.

She has joined her loved ones gone on before
And waits for us to enter Heavens door
There we too shall live forever more.

Precious memories she leaves behind
That shall be forever recessed in our heart and mind
With chords of love that sweetly bind!

SHOW ME SWEET JESUS

Dear Jesus, hold me
Ever close to your side;
I need your love within my heart
To forever abide.

Show me Sweet Jesus
Thy own perfect will and way.
My path gets lonely
I need you right now, today.

Fill my heart with love, Holy One
And let it overflow.
I want to be one in thee
So your amazing love I can show.

Take my hand Precious Jesus
And be my guide.
I am tired and weary
I need you ever near my side.

Hold me, my Wonderful Savior
Take away my bent for sinning.
Fill this empty cup of mine
Help me make a new beginning.

Guide me, Gracious Lord
To some lost soul today.
Show me, Sweet Jesus
How to lead them thy way!

SHOW ME THE WAY LORD

Lord, bind me next to the heart of thine
Wrap me tight with thy holy twine
Show me the way; give me a sign
Lighten this dreary path of mine.

Lord, your love thrills me so
I need it as thru life I go.
Take this fainting heart of mine
Fill it with thy grace and mercy divine.

Lord, hear me as I pray
I seek your will night and day.
My faith in you will never die
And your love always lifts me high.

Lord, I'm just a sinner seeking your grace
You are my most sacred hiding place.
Lift me up and help me stand
Until I meet you face to face in heaven's land!

SING OF JESUS' BIRTH

Oh' sing all people
Sing of the Christ child's birth.
Peace and good will He brought
Down from heaven to earth.

He's God's Son; Jesus is His name
And He, the Lamb of God, took all blame.
Give Him glory and praise
He, our Savior, can mend our broken ways.

Oh' sing and praise His name
The world will never be the same.
He can save the vilest sinner thru His grace
His birth and death made the world a better place!

SING UNTO GOD

You're God's Child; so unto Him sing
Lift up your voice; let it joyfully ring.
When His children sing, great joy to Him it doth bring
He is worthy since He's your Savior and King.

Glorify and praise His holy name
Let the world know He bore all blame.
Your heart will rejoice in knowing
That unto others your faith you're showing.

Have a grateful heart for God's love
Let your soul sing out to Him above.
Be dedicated to Him in glorification and song
He's your Redeemer who can do no wrong.

Praise Him in glorification as the Holy One
He is the Great and Mighty, God's own Son.
He's the Prince of Peace who gives Salvation free
And has prepared a place for us to live eternally!

SOMEDAY SOON

Someday soon our toiling on earth will be done
We'll come face to face with Jesus, the holy one
He will hold us near since our final race will be run.

Someday soon peace and joy will flood our soul
Jesus will renew our body and make us whole
In Heavens land where He is the light and has control.

Someday soon all our heartaches will be gone
There will be no more sin and turmoil to condone
Jesus, our Savior, will claim us as His own.

Someday soon we'll meet God far above the skies
We'll behold the Promised Land thru delightful eyes
And there'll be no more goodbyes.

Someday soon we'll feel the touch of God's hand
And walk on streets of gold serenaded by the angel band
Our hearts will swell with joy as we peruse Heavens land.

Someday soon we'll be reunited with loved ones gone on before
We'll have a joyous jubilee in that sweet land of yore
While praising God, the Holy One, for His blessings galore!

SONGS IN THE NIGHT

God gives me songs in the night
To shed His good and perfect light
His glory shines luminous and bright.

Songs in the night so melodiously sweet
Words of wisdom given to me to repeat
They make me strong when I'm weak.

Yea' God gives me songs in the night
That lifts my spirit to a loftier height
They fill my heart with joy and delight.

Songs in the night given by God to extol
They enter my mind, body and soul
To heal my broken spirit and make me whole!

SPRING IS HERE

Spring is in the air
Trees blossom in beauty fair.
Plants pop up from the sod
New life is being reborn by God.

Birds are beautiful in their splendor
As they fly right past my window,
They stop at my bird feeders in grand array
Where they spend most of the day.

Gone are winters drab coats
A balmy fragrance softly floats,
Within the warming atmosphere
As buds and blossoms pop out everywhere.

It's a time of renewal and rebirth
For plants and trees all across the earth.
God, the Master Creator, enhances all our lands
With the awesome touch of His powerful hands!

STAY NEAR ME LORD

Lord, there's no place I'd rather be
Than sheltered in the arms of thee.
You're the keeper of my heart and soul
Your grace and love make me whole.

Lord, keep walking close by my side
Beneath thy wings of love, I want to hide.
There's no way I could keep going without you
I need your love so proud and true.

Lord, take this weary heart of mine
Make it beat with yours in time.
Let thy threads of love intertwine
To make it more like thine.

Lord, I'm just a sinner begging for grace
I yearn to reach thy heavenly place.
I offer you my heart, body and soul
It is yours forever; I give you complete control!

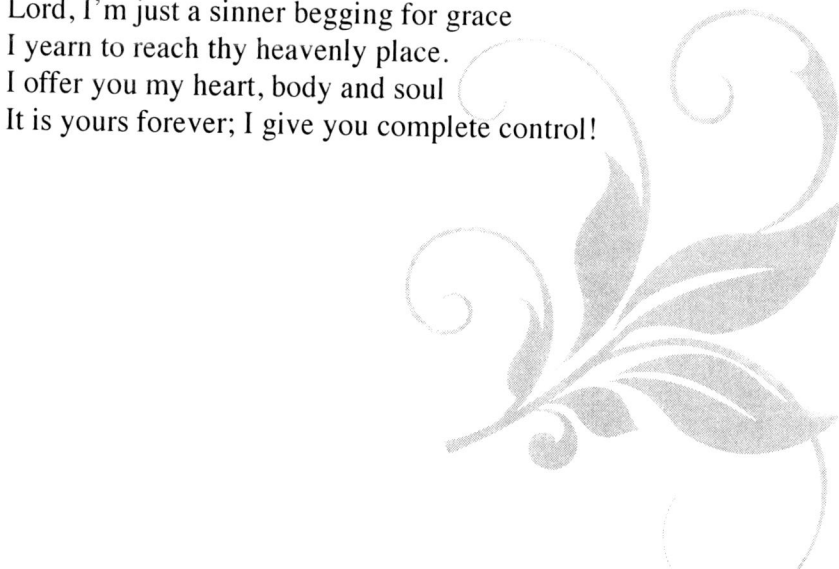

SURRENDER TO THE LORD

Surrender your soul to the Lord
He will fill your heart with sweet accord.
He will freely share His love divine
And bind you next to Him with holy twine.

The only way to reach God is thru Jesus, His Son
Who total victory over our sin won,
When He shed His blood on the cross at Calvary
To wash away our sins and set us free.

Never tarry by the wayside or attempt to wait
Accept Jesus as your Savior before it's too late.
He died a cruel death for all of our sins to atone
Now and forever He gives Salvation, the greatest gift ever known!

SWEET ETERNITY

Hallelujah, praise the name of our Lord
He is our Savior who is to be adored.
Sing unto Him, our Redeemer, in admiration
He freely gave His life to give us salvation.

There is none other as loving as He
He bore our sins on the cross at Calvary
Shedding His precious blood to set us free
So we may forever ransomed be.

Jesus, Son of God, saved us thru His grace
Thru amazing love, He died in our place.
He arose from death and the grave in victory
Now and forever He offers sweet eternity.

Jesus ascended to heaven to reign with God His Father above
There He intervenes with Him for you and me thru love.
Glorify Him for giving salvation and loving us so much
He healed our broken spirit with His awesome touch!

SWEET HOLY SPIRIT

Sweet Holy Spirit
Hold me ever near.
Whisper to me softly
Words of love so clear.

Live within my heart
Your winsome ways to impart.
Take this troubled soul of mine
Make it thy own by design.

Sweet Holy Spirit
Cast my troubles away.
Keep me within thy sight
Never more to stray.

I'm merely a sinner
Saved by God's grace.
Guide me with thy hand
Until I finish my earthly race!

THANKFUL FOR THE LAMB

I am so thankful for the Lamb
Who made me what I am.
I shall forever worship Him
He lights my path when dim.

I am so thankful for the Lamb
He loved me in the highest degree;
And gave His life to ransom me
On the cross at Calvary.

I am so thankful for the precious Lamb
He is my Savior and the Great I Am.
He offers me salvation and eternity
Thru His amazing grace and love so free.

I am so thankful for the Lamb
He's my Master, Savior and friend
On whom I can always depend
My love for Him will never end.

The Lamb of God holds my hand
As I travel thru this perilous land
And gives me the strength to stand
As I follow Him and obey His command!

THANKING GOD FOR SALVATION

I bow in humble admiration
Thanking God for my salvation.
My soul rejoices deep within
Knowing Jesus, God's Son, took away my sin.

Jesus bore the cross to save my soul
He shed His precious blood to make me whole.
I shall always praise Him and forever thankful be
That He cared so much for a sinner like me.

Jesus loved me more than words can tell
He rescued me from Satan's clutches and hell.
Through love He paved my way to glory land
There I shall make my great and final stand!

THE ANGEL BAND

In heaven's glorious land
There's an angel band,
That treads on streets of gold
They are a majestic sight to behold.

Their voices joyfully ring
In praises to Christ our King.
They stand united in a band
Claiming Jesus as their brand.

They chant holy, holy to the Lord
As they march in sweet accord.
While the trumpet softly plays
Melodious voices they raise.

The angel band is right inside Heaven's door
So they can bid us welcome forevermore,
To God's beautiful city of light
Where there is no darkness or night!

THE DIVINE BRIDGE

The sole bridge to save us was built by God
With two timbers in the form of the cross.
The only hands that can rescue us
Were nailed to the cross so we would not be lost.

We cannot be saved apart from grace
It is a gift given freely by God thru the death of His Son.
Only when we realize our utter helplessness
May we receive the gift and victory over sin be won.

Grace is what we stand on today
When we sin, grace takes our guilt away.
When we are weak, God's grace makes us strong
When we are tempted, grace lets us know right from wrong.

Grace unites our heart in this perilous world
It gives us strength to resist Satan's darts when hurled.
Grace guides us in a Godly direction
With Jesus, as our Savior, it gives us direct connection!

THE GREATEST FRIEND EVER KNOWN

Dear Jesus, I'm so thankful I have you
When heartaches arise you're near for me to turn to.

Thank you for your never ending love
And the many blessings you send from above.

On your amazing love my heart and soul depends
Like a beautiful dove on me it constantly descends.

You're the greatest friend I've ever known
As long as I have you I'll never walk alone!

THE HEAVENLY STAIRWAY

There's a heavenly stairway that we must climb
Doing our best to avoid all sin and grime,
If we want to feel the love of Jesus, our Savior, Divine
It's straight and narrow; so just take your time.

You must follow the steps of Jesus as He leads
Your hungry soul with His Manna He feeds;
He knows your heartaches and satisfies your needs
He is anxious to see that all of His children succeeds.

Make it a goal to climb the heavenly stairway
Work toward going to heaven each day;
Dedicate your life to Jesus; He will show you the way
Lift your heart and soul to Him and pray!

THE JOURNEY TO HEAVEN

The journey to heaven is an upward climb
With many rough places filled with grime.
Just hold Jesus' hand; He'll help you along
His love and grace will make you brave and strong.

At times the path is winding and rough
But our Saviors love is always enough;
He will walk beside us to give hope
And whisper words of encouragement to help us cope.

Jesus always knows exactly where we are
He strives to be our shining star.
He brings us from darkness into His light
To assure that we win old Satan's fight.

If we should falter by the way
All we have to do is lift our voice and pray.
Jesus stays near for us to call on
So we will never have to walk alone.

Many times Jesus sends angels in disguise
Just to help us along and open our eyes.
They come with wings unfurled
To carry us thru trials of this world!

THE KEEPER OF MY HEART

Lord, I know I am a sinner
This is my earnest plea.
Purge my sins away
Purify the heart of me.

Lord, I couldn't make it in life
If not for the love of you.
When I'm in deep distress
You quickly come to my rescue.

Lord, you give me comfort
And courage when I have none.
Just walk ever near me
Until life on earth is done.

Lord, you're the keeper of my heart
I give the key to only you.
There's no one on earth
Who loves me the way you do.

Lord, hold me close
Fill this cup of mine.
Take my trembling heart
Make it beat with yours in time!

THE LORD IS MY EVERYTHING

Lord, you're my everything
You make my heart with joy sing
Rich blessings to my life you bring.

I never have to doubt your love
It's far better than I've ever dreamed of
It lifts me to loftier heights above.

Lord, I can't fathom where I would be
If not for the amazing grace of thee
Your love has set my soul forever free.

Lord, I give you all glory and praise
For your wondrous and winsome ways
You set my heart and soul ablaze!

THE LORD IS MY HOPE FOR ETERNITY

Thank you Lord for the gift of another day
May I glorify you in all that I do and say?
Lord, I know you have made me your own
I rejoice in your presence and will never be alone.

Lord you are awesome and worthy of my praise
I will worship you in spirit and truth always.
I surrender my all to you whose love is true
Take my life as an offering to you.

Lord I acknowledge that I need you
Control my actions my life to renew.
I worship you in the beauty of your holiness
And long to feel your loving caress.

Lord I acknowledge my need for thee
You are my hope for sweet eternity.
Let thy truth and peace guard my mind
Within the power of thy cross great solstice I find.

Lord thru thy blood you have accepted me
Your compassion and grace has set me free.
Create in me a heart that longs for you
You are my salvation and Redeemer so true!

THE MASTER OF DIVINITY

Let Jesus come into your heart
He will give you a brand new start.
His cleansing power will take your sins away
And He will change your darkest night to day.

Jesus wants to live deep within your soul
With love your actions He will control.
He is the great and mighty Master of Divinity
Who can make you what you ought to be.

Jesus' love will serve you well
He will rescue you from Satan and hell.
Accept Him and follow Him this very day
He will lead you the heavenly way!

THE SOUL SHALL NEVER DIE

Lord, you've taken our loved one thru the clouds on high
Where Jesus is the light and the soul shall never die
You make no mistakes but it's so hard for us to say goodbye
Although we know we will meet again in the sweet by and by!

We realize for each of our lives you have a special plan
Someday soon you'll take us gently by the hand
And lead us home to your beautiful promised land
Where we shall make our great and final stand!

Thru your power and grace our body you will renew
Then we will stroll on streets of gold forever more with you.
There will be a great homecoming in your sweet land up there
Everyone will be safe and secure in your love and care.

There will be no pain and suffering and not a burden will we bear
Scores of angels will be commanded to linger near.
Our spirit will join in with the Heavenly jubilee
As we meet on the shore of Heaven's crystal sea.

Life is fleeting; our time to go may be only a heartbeat away
We must be ready to meet you when you call on our final day.
We'll always treasure memories made down thru the years
Sweet Savior and Comforter hold us tight as we shed our tears.

Lord, help us stay ready for our final call
Lift us high toward heaven's table land never more to fall
Help us cross over your beautiful Heavenly wall
We wait to meet our loved ones at our great and final call!

THE TOUCH OF HIS HAND

Look for Jesus, the Great I Am
Feel the touch of His hand.
With His amazing love
Your soul He will brand.

Walk with Jesus, the Holy One
Marvel at the touch of His hand.
Through life's trials
He will help you stand.

Depend on Jesus, our Redeemer
Joyfully receive the touch of His hand.
He will lead you ever so gently
As you travel thru this weary land.

Praise Jesus, our Savior
Thrill to the touch of His hand.
He will stay close beside you
Glorify Him and follow His command.

Cling tight to Jesus, the Lamb of God
Thank Him for the touch of His hand.
He will take you home to Heaven
Where there is no sinking sand!

THE WHIPPOORWILLS

Early last night I heard a lone whippoorwill
His call vibrated across the hill.
It came from the valley below
Down by the stream where cool waters flow.

I stepped outside to listen in awe
He called out continuously without a flaw.
Suddenly a call vibrated back to him
It came from a distance low and dim.

Soon the calls came closer together than before
They sounded as if right outside my back door.
Then the night became quiet and still
I guess that's the way of a whippoorwill.

Through his calls he had located a mate
That's how whippoorwills communicate.
Away through the moon lit sky they flew
On a mission to do whatever whippoorwills do!

THERE IS PEACE WITH JESUS

There is a peace that I know
It comes from Jesus who loves me so.
All I have to do is seek His face
To be blest by His amazing grace.

Jesus forgave me of my sin
He shined His love light to my soul within.
He is my hope and salvation
And is the reason for my transformation.

Jesus' love outshines the sun
His love is available for everyone.
Just believe in Him and seek His face
He'll get you in the heavenly race.

Jesus will guard your heart and mind
With his love so proud and true.
Within the balm of His love you'll find
He will change your life through and through!

THROW OUT THE LIFELINE

Let your love light shine
Reflecting Jesus' love divine
Throw out the lifeline.

Let everyone see Jesus in you
Share love in all that you do
Be a lighthouse for others to view.

Work diligently souls to save
Be strong in faith; be bold and brave
Throw out the lifeline; someone's path to heaven pave!

TRUST GOD

God is your shield and defender
His strength and love to you He doth render.
When all of your strength is gone
He offers His arms for you to lean on.

God's strength is sufficient for your needs
Trust Him and follow Him where He leads.
Surrender your heart and soul to Him
And all worldly things will grow dim.

God holds your life in His hands
Your life with love He freely brands.
Accept and enjoy the peace He offers you
Be spiritually minded and glorify Him in all you do!

UNCHANGING LOVE

God's love is unchanging
Over sin He gives victory.
He, our Lord, is all powerful
His grace and mercy He offers free.

Put your trust in God day and night
He will lift you to your loftiest height.
Take joy in praising Him along the way
Kneel in humble admiration to Him and pray.

God is honorable and worthy of your praise
If you trust Him, He will bless your days.
His unchanging love is awesome and free
It paves the way to Heavenly Eternity!

WALK WITH ME LORD

Lord, draw me nearer to thee
Hold me close until thy blessed face I see
There's no other place I'd rather be.

Take this fainting heart of mine
Fill it with thy love divine
My body and soul is yours to refine.

Lord, reach into my life with thy loving hand
Impart your will and way; take complete command
Lead me in paths where there's no sinking sand.

Touch my life to blot out all shame and sin
Shine thy majestic glory deep within
Walk with me daily as a new life I begin!

WALK WITHIN GOD'S LIGHT OF LOVE

The pearly gates are open wide
God invites you to come inside.
He will welcome you with open arms
And protect you from all harms.

God sent us His Son, Jesus, to offer salvation free
There is none other as great as He.
Accept Him as your Savior, Lord and King
Your heart with joyful rapture will sing.

Walk within the divine light of God's love
He gives satisfactions you've never dreamed of.
Look unto Him for guidance from day to day
He will pave your path to heaven never more to stray!

WE BELONG TO GOD

Be still and hear what God has to say
He wants to live in your heart and take your sin away
Seek to perceive what He wants you to do each day.

We belong to God; He claims us as His own
His Son, Jesus, shed His blood for our sins to atone
We are the sheep of His pasture and He'll never leave us alone.

God accepts us when we believe in Him and saves us thru His grace
When we pray, God wraps us in His arms in a loving embrace
He is always near; we can count on Him to be every place.

God is our most intimate and treasured friend
He's our Savior and our broken ways He will mend
He assures us on His grace and love we can depend!

WHAT A GLORIOUS DAY

Today I knelt down beside the goldenrod
On the pond dam where weeping willows nod
Just to have a little talk with God.

I was troubled and needed a friend
Someone who my broken spirit would mend
I knew on God's grace and love I could depend.

God descended to show how much He loved me
And assured me His love would forever be
From my troubles He, my Savior, set me free.

When I got up to leave
He touched me softly on my sleeve
And told me His grace was mine to receive.

Oh' what a glorious and perfect day
God took my heartaches and troubles away
His divine love and mercy blessed me more than I can say!

WHEN I AM GONE

When I'm gone, please shed no tears for me
I'll be home with Jesus for eternity
And we will have a heavenly jubilee.

I will meet my loved ones gone on before
Together we will share heavenly treasures galore
Our hearts and souls with joy will soar.

Just keep your faith in Jesus strong
And I'll see you again before too long
Then together we will sing a sweet, sweet song.

There's great comfort in knowing
Where you are eventually going
When it's to that fair land with milk and honey flowing.

Treasure the precious memories we have shared
And our love for each other showing how much we cared
Put your trust in Jesus and keep your heart and soul prepared.

God waits with open arms to welcome you in
To His beautiful haven of rest where there is no sin
Perfect peace and love shall reign forever therein!

WINGS OF LOVE

Lord, carry me away
To a much fairer day,
On wings of endless love
To abide with you in heaven above.

I'll gladly leave my burdens behind
So true peace and love I may find.
Perfect is the peace that you impart
As earthly sorrows end and heavens joys start.

Lord, your love means everything to me
And I know it shall last throughout eternity.
Though dark clouds gather and fierce winds blow
I'll press forward and onward go.

Within thy grace I will forever stand
And cling tightly to thy nail scarred hand.
So just fly me on wings of love in sweet refrain
Where there'll be no more heartache or pain!

WORSHIP JESUS IN HIS DEITY

When the battles of the world let you down
And in a sea of misery you almost drown,
Reach out for Jesus and take His hand
He will lift you up and help you stand.

On your darkest days Jesus is always there
Willing and waiting to hear your prayer.
He will relieve your heartaches to brighten your days
He will mend your broken ways.

Jesus stands ready to hear your call
He will make you stand proud and tall.
His amazing grace and love He offers you
Call on Him and He will see you through.

Jesus prompts us to worship Him in His deity
And praise Him for the entire world to see.
He uses our praise to draw others to Him
So He can bless them with eternal life in heavens realm!

WORSHIP THE ALMIGHTY KING OF KINGS

Fall down on your knees and pray
Seek the Lord and Savior today
He stands ready to light your way.

Glorify Him for His goodness
His light will blot out all your darkness
Walk within His light and onward press.

Bountiful blessings unto you He brings
Worship Him as Almighty King of Kings
He will shelter you beneath His wings.

For all of your sins our Savior did atone
And He will never leave you alone
He is the Great I Am and the best friend ever known!

YOUR LIFELINE CRUTCH

Look around and you will see
Wondrous works of God in His deity
From the smallest blade of grass to the tallest tree.

There's the majestic beauty of the rose
With the mystery of how God unfolds it as it buds and grows
Thru awesome powers that only He knows.

Look at all the beautiful flowers
And the butterflies that visit them for hours
Until chased away by the summer showers.

Feel the sunshine as it daily kisses your face
It is sent by God in His awesome grace
To light your path as thru life on earth you race.

When each day is over and done
Feast your eyes on the beauty of the setting sun
With magnificent colors so pleasing to look upon.

Watch the birds as from tree to tree they fly
See the silver clouds as they float serenely by
Look upon moonlights luminous glow and the starry sky.

Climb mountains and walk by the seashore
Hear the waves as they crash and roar
Watch the sea gulls as they soar.

Feel the cool breeze and its soothing touch
And know that God loves you very much
His amazing never ending love is your lifeline crutch!

YOUR REDEEMER AND FRIEND

Believe in Jesus who paves the way
To His heavenly home never more to stray.
Priceless and wonderful it is
When we walk in the steps of His.

Sing of his mercies and praise His name
He's our Savior who took all blame.
He offered us salvation pure and true
When He gave His life to give us life anew.

Share the beautiful story
Of how Jesus came in His glory.
Tell of His love and amazing grace
As through this hectic life you race.

Feed on His holy word
Your soul with His Armor He will gird.
Feast on His blessings that He doth send
Claim Him as your Redeemer and Friend!

Other published books are:

Inspirational And Tranquil Moments

Heavenly Inspirations

Walking With My Savior

Inspirations To Heal The Soul.

CPSIA information can be obtained
at www.ICGtesting.com
Printed in the USA
FFOW01n1448160916
27701FF